TROUT AND SALMON FLY INDEX

Dick Surette

Revised and Enlarged Edition

STACKPOLE BOOKS

TROUT AND SALMON FLY INDEX
Copyright © 1978 by Dick Surette

Published by
STACKPOLE BOOKS
Cameron and Kelker Streets
P.O. Box 1831
Harrisburg, Pa. 17105

Published simultaneously in Don Mills, Ontario, Canada
by Thomas Nelson & Sons, Ltd.

The drawings on pages 10 to 23 are by John Noga.

Printed in the U.S.A.

Library of Congress Cataloging in Publication Data
Surette, Dick, 1935–
    Trout and salmon fly index.

    Includes index.
    1. Flies, Artificial. 2. Fly tying. I. Title.
II. Title: Salmon fly index.
SH451.S87   688.7′9   78-24196
ISBN 0-8117-2093-4

688.7
Sur

CONTENTS

64867

HOW TO TIE BASIC FLIES

This section will serve as a basic guide to the construction of all types of flies. We will tie the bucktail, streamer, wet, nymph, dry, bass bug, Atlantic salmon and the jig. Practically all flies can be mastered once you learn the principles of fly tying on the above types of flies. The only difference among patterns is the choice of different materials and hooks with some minor changes.

This is not a complete course in fly tying, for the field is complex. This book is geared to the beginner who seeks a simple, clear guide using a photograph and caption approach to get started on fly tying. As you progress and refine your tying, you will want to delve into the subject thoroughly. But first things first: the basic principles of fly construction are herein contained.

Any fly really has only two essential qualities: it should catch fish, and secondly, it should hold together and be durable. Even poorly tied flies will get fish but they fall apart after short usage, a frustrating event for the fellow who has found a killer fly. A finished fly should be neat, tight, and proportioned in relation to hook size, not overdressed or underdressed.

I can still recall the thrill of accomplishment when I first landed a 7-inch brookie on my first Quill Gordon over 26 years ago. The same feeling swept over me a few years ago with my first salmon in New Brunswick and it will probably come again if I ever get out west to fish for steelhead.

The practicality of being able to tie your own flies can not be underestimated. You will save money, a most important factor today, and you will never be caught short on a correct pattern or the ability to match the hatch you saw the previous day but could not find in your local tackle store. You will be surprised to find how imaginative and creative you can be when given the chance. If you can tie your shoes you can tie flies. Some will develop into superb tyers, others to a lesser degree but all will have enjoyment and satisfaction. What else could you ask?

—DICK SURETTE

TOOLS

The single most important tool is the vise. A good vise will last a lifetime for the average tyer and the best your pocket can afford is a buy that you will not regret. The vise should hold the fly securely and tightly so the hook will not move while the fly is being tied. The jaws of the vise should be tapered to hold small hooks easily and properly with little or no adjustment.

There are just two basic styles of vises, the stationary and rotary vise. The stationary vise stays in a fixed position and you will tie all fly patterns in this position. The rotary vise allows the tyer to rotate the fly and hold the materials steady and spin them on the hook as he turns the vise. All vises should hold hooks from size 4/0 to 24 securely without much adjustment. Remember you only get what you pay for. Vises range from $2.00 to $150.

The next most often used tool is a good pair of scissors. They should have large finger holes and fine points for trimming and cutting. You may want a second pair for cutting rough materials and difficult items; these can be of lesser quality. Save your best scissors for tying only. Curved or straight points will do the job perfectly. I have a pair I used constantly for fifteen years, sending them out once a year for overhaul and sharpening. Scissors range from $2.00 to $10.00.

A pair of hackle pliers is next on the list. These are used to attach hackles or other types of materials to flies. They will grasp small feathers and hold them securely while you wind the material on the fly—most helpful. The pliers are shaped so that pressure will open the jaws to grab material and releasing the pressure on the pliers will hold the material. Some are rubber-tipped and some have serrated jaws. If you find that they cut feathers, dull the jaws somewhat on a piece of wood to remove burr. Hackle pliers range from $1.00 to $4.00.

A bodkin is simply a needle inserted into a handle. One end may have a hole for tying a half hitch knot—very handy. The bodkin will be useful in applying glue to heads of flies, picking out fur-dubbed bodies, and doing a host of other jobs. Keep the point sharp and clean. Price range 60 cents to $2.00.

A bobbin is used to hold the thread and is like a third hand—very important. The bobbin always keeps some tension on the fly while it is being tied and helps to keep the fly tight. Most bobbins are pressure-sensitive and hold the thread by pressure from the sides. Be careful not to get a burr on the barrel for it will continually break your thread. Price range $2.00 to $5.00.

These are basic tools for starters.

MATERIALS AND HOOKS

Once again the key is quality. A good builder would never use inferior lumber; in order to have a superior fly you need good materials. You will find that the gathering and selection of materials is one of the most interesting parts of tying—even the neighbor's collie all of a sudden looks like Light Cahill material. It will take many years to become a good buyer of materials. This pursuit of materials is never-ending for new materials will come along and you will have to decide whether they measure up to your own likes and dislikes. Much of this is personal and that is perfectly all right; you should feel most confident in this skill.

Very often price is the best indicator of quality. Nobody sells a $20.00 shirt for $1.00 and the same is true with fly tying materials. Many items can be picked up at church bazaars, auctions and or by just plain rummaging around in the house or attic. Often you will see animals—muskrats, beavers, foxes—that have been run over on the highway. Stop! Put the animal in a bag and bring him home to be skinned, then bury the carcass. You've cleaned the highway and also found some free materials. Don't forget your hunter friends. Trade flies for the feathers, skins, tails and other results of their success in hunting. Don't waste any item!

Build your supply slowly and plan each purchase to be a permanent choice. All mail-order houses are anxious to please their customers. If it is not what you expected, return it and they will be more than happy to help you.

In regards to hooks, the Mustad Company of Norway is the most dependable source of hooks in the world. The hook is a most integral part of any fly. Quality materials and good technique on poor hooks waste the fly tyers' time. The variety of hooks is never ending

—lengths, strengths, bends, and eyes in all sorts of styles. Mustad sells hooks all over the world and usually keeps them in good supply throughout the year. They are the most consistent.

You would do well to stock few styles of hooks but a wide variety of sizes to fill your needs. The most economical way is by boxes of one hundred. Get a buddy to split an order of hooks with you; this way each will get fifty hooks of one size and style.

In hook sizes, the larger the number the smaller the hook, so size 22 is very small and size 8 is large. For a basic stock consider the following as a guideline: Mustad #94840 for dry fly in sizes 8, 10, 12, 14, 16, 18, 20, 22. Mustad #3906 for wet fly in sizes 10, 12, 14, 16. Mustad #3665A for streamers and bucktails in sizes 4, 6, 8, 10, 12 and Mustad #38941 for nymphs in sizes 6, 8, 10, 12, 14. You do not need all of these hooks at once, but you should build up your stock in this progression. This is meant to be a guideline to a basic inventory tested by time and trout for many years by many fly tyers.

Wools, feathers, hair, threads, furs, and now synthetics make up the greatest supply of available materials. Do not be stumped if the dressing calls for the whiskers of an African dodo—use the same texture and color and substitute with your most similar materials and you will be surprised.

Below are some actual samples of some of the Mustad line of fly tying hooks. This will give you a rough idea of hook sizes and proportions.

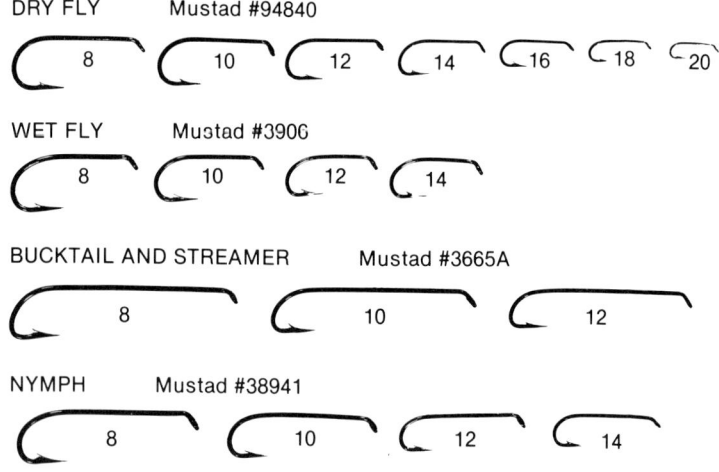

DRY FLY   Mustad #94840

8   10   12   14   16   18   20

WET FLY   Mustad #3906

8   10   12   14

BUCKTAIL AND STREAMER   Mustad #3665A

8   10   12

NYMPH   Mustad #38941

8   10   12   14

There are many other types and styles. These are shown to give you a basic inventory of hooks.

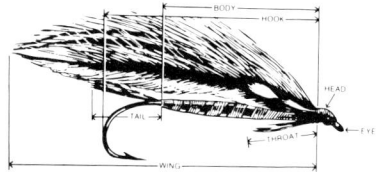

SIZES AND PARTS OF
BUCKTAIL AND STREAMER

Tail = ⅓ length of body
Wing = ⅓ longer than hook
Body = length of shank
Throat = ⅓ length of body

SIZES AND PARTS OF
WET FLY

Tail = length of wings
Wings = length of hook plus
Hackles = ½ length of body
Body = length of shank

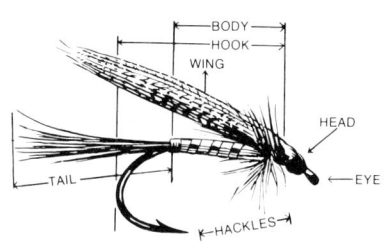

SIZES AND PARTS OF
THE NYMPH

Tail = Abdomen
Abdomen = ⅔ body
Legs = length of thorax
Thorax = ⅓ of body

SIZES AND PARTS OF
THE DRY FLY

Tail = Body
Body = length of shank
Wings = length of body
Hackle = ¾ length of wings

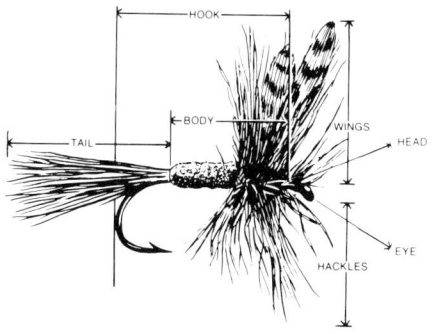

9

BUCKTAILS

A bucktail is usually the easiest fly for the beginner to tie. The wing is usually hair—bucktail, impali, woodchuck, fitch or any other coarse hair will be fine. Wing materials should be tied sparsely to allow the fly to pulsate or breathe as it is retrieved. The color combinations and variety are endless, so use your imagination. All flies fall into two basic styles: the bright, colorful attractor such as the Mickey Finn; or drab, somber copies of food forms such as the Black Nose Dace. We will tie the Mickey Finn.

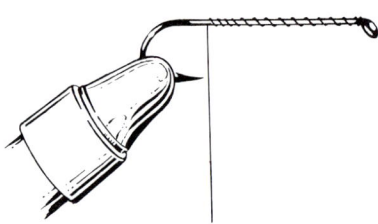

1. Place a streamer hook in vise as shown. You must hold the hook securely and firmly but not so tight that you take the temper out of the hook or break the hook itself. Never cover the point of the hook with the vise. Begin all flies by wrapping thread over the entire shank of the hook. This provides a base for all future fly tying operations.

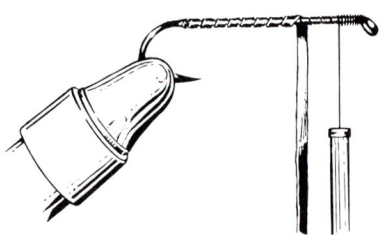

2. Use flat silver tinsel for body. We will double wrap the body, that is, wrap two layers of tinsel. Begin at front of hook, wrap neatly to bend, come back to starting point. Leave plenty of room for a good neat head—it is a primary problem for all tyers to leave enough room to finish the head properly.

3. The Mickey Finn has two colors, red and yellow. Tie a small bunch of yellow bucktail directly on top. Make the first turn a holding turn, then on subsequent turns really bear down to hold bucktail firmly.

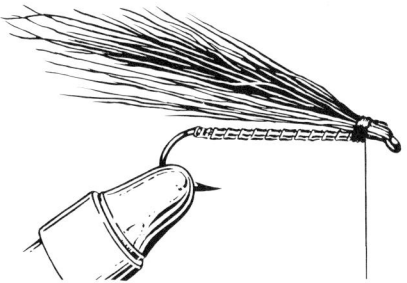

4. Add the red bucktail over the yellow, then cut all materials at this point on a taper to build up a neat tapered head, the sign of a well-tied fly.

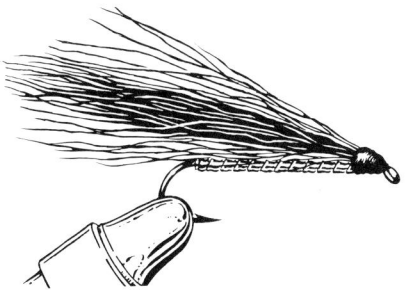

5. Next step is to add the yellow once more. The fly is now ready for winding down the yellow bucktail. The final step is to use a series of half hitch knots to form a secure head. Use this knot for all flies as the last step. Add black lacquer; use three or four light applications. Here we have a neat, sparse, balanced fly that will catch trout anywhere in the world.

STREAMERS

A streamer is very similar to a bucktail except the wing material is usually a feather wing as compared to the hair wing on the bucktail. A maribou wing fits into the streamer category. Streamers are most effective when fished deep on the bottom of the pond, lake or stream early and late in the season. Our streamer will be the Black Ghost, a fly originated in Maine over fifty years ago.

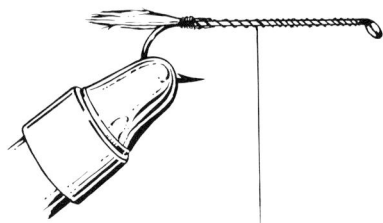

1. Attach hook in vise same as in bucktail. Attach yellow fibers for tail, usually saddle hackle barbules or cock neck barbules. Do not make tail too long for this will encourage unwanted short strikes.

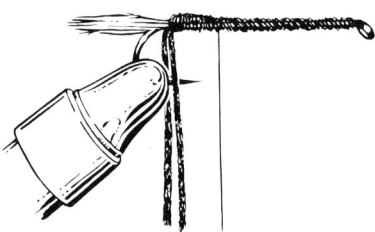

2. Attach flat silver tinsel securely. This will be wound on later as ribbing material. Attach black body silk and wind it in for the full length of hook for a good, tight body.

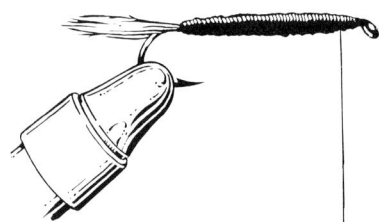

3. Wrap black silk body, taper and build up as shown in the photo. When winding body materials, always position the thread at the finish or tie-in spot before beginning.

4. Wrap silver tinsel over body in neat spirals. This is the ribbing and will add a bit of flash to the fly. Body is now complete. Add a bit of yellow barbules for throat.

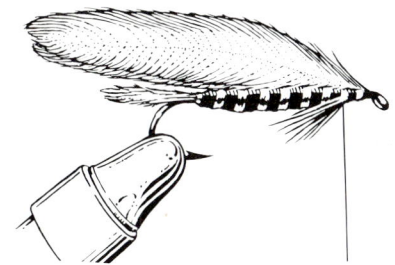

5. Select four white saddle hackles of good shape and length. Place concave sides together and tie on top as in photo. Leave room for head and be careful of length of wing; too long will give you short strikes.

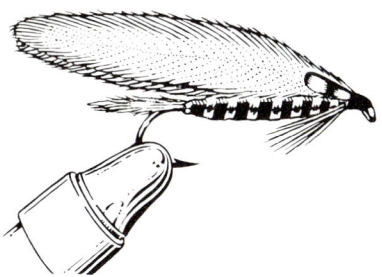

6. Add jungle cock eye. You will have to use a synthetic jungle cock eye for this is no longer available in its natural form. Cut all materials carefully and complete head. Put on three or four coats of black lacquer to finish. On all streamers be most careful not to tie the wing materials too long as they will tend to wrap around the hook causing the fly to ride improperly and the fish to strike short at the fly.

13

WETS

Wet flies are the oldest form of artificial flies and are used under the surface of the water like bucktails and streamers. Most wets resemble the immature forms of insects that live in an aquatic environment. When these nymphs mature and move from the depths to the surface, this we call a hatch. Bright wets are again just colorful attractor type patterns. Our wet fly will be the Royal Coachman, tied in the 1830's in England and brought to the American continent by the colonists.

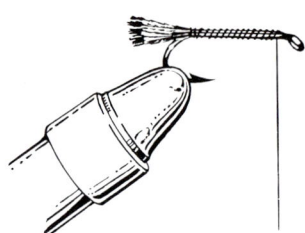

1. Secure a wet fly hook in vise, wrap thread to bend of hook. Attach golden pheasant tippets for tail, tie in full length of body down shank of hook. Do not cut material short for this will cause a bump in the body. Keep this in mind for all flies. Tie all excess into the body as much as possible.

2. Body is three parts: one part peacock herl, one part red silk and one part peacock herl. Attach as in photo.

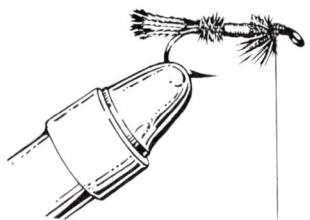

3. Tie in brown hackle. Wrap two or three turns and tie back over hackle to form collar style. Use soft hackle or dry fly hackle, tied very sparsely.

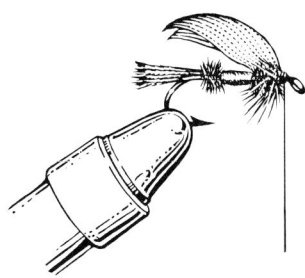

4. Select two white duck or white goose quills, one right and one left wing quill. Cut a small piece from each of the long sides of the quill, staying away from the very top and the very bottom of the quill which are difficult to use for wing materials. Place the cut wing quill pieces, concave sides together, directly on top of the fly. Take one turn with the thread, usually size 4/0 to 6/0, for hook sizes 8 to 16. This will hold wings in place so you can see if the wings sit properly on the fly. Add further turns of thread to secure the wings permanently.

5. Complete the fly by wrapping thread several turns to form a neat and compact head. Use three or four coats of lacquer to secure and cement the head. Keep eye of the fly free from excess lacquer, which is most frustrating if you cannot thread the leader through the eye of the fly. Prewaxed nylon is an excellent small diameter thread for all wets, drys and nymphs in the smaller sizes. The thread color can be coordinated with the basic color of the fly for a nicely-tied fly. Almost all wet flies are tied in this basic format though the colors, materials and size may change from pattern to pattern.

HINT: Always begin your angling with a wet fly if no fish can be seen rising. If you can not see them feeding, they must be feeding under the surface as they do for 80 to 90 percent of the time.

NYMPHS

The nymph style of fly is a recent refinement of the wet fly being shaped more like the natural insect. This is a good fly style to master, nymph fishing being the most challenging but also most rewarding to those who master the system. The nymph we will tie is the Montana Stonefly and again we will utilize the rotary vise.

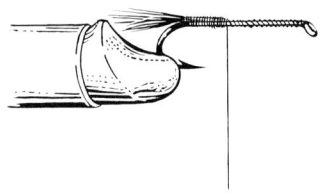

1. Place hook in vise, wrap thread on shank of hook, use black hackle barbules for tail.

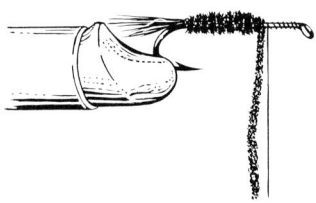

2. Attach black chenille, spin vise clockwise with left hand and guide chenille onto hook. This forms the abdomen. Leave a short piece to tie in the cover, which is the black top part of the thorax.

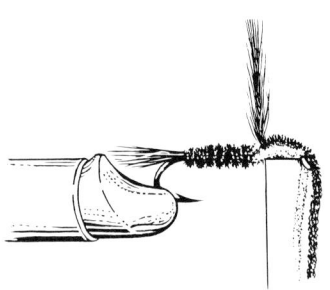

3. Attach black hackle and yellow chenille for building up thorax or the front portion of the nymph. This should be much larger than the abdomen.

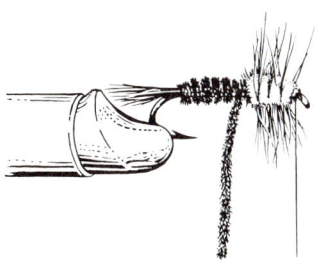

4. Wind yellow chenille in place on thorax. Rib thorax with black hackle. Cut both yellow chenille and black hackle. Trim both top and bottom of fly.

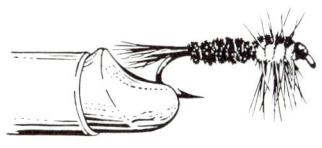

5. Bring black chenille covert over top portion of thorax, cut, and apply lacquer as in prior flies.

HINTS: Fur dubbed nymphs are excellent types of flies. Take a soft fur—rabbit, muskrat, possum, badger, etc.—and SPARINGLY apply fur over pre-waxed nylon as it hangs down from your bobbin. Spin bobbin with your left hand clockwise. Spin fur clockwise with your right hand over the thread, using your thumb and index finger of the right hand. You can spin any size fur body from size 2 to size 22. Furs can be easily blended to get the exact color for the tone of the fly. You can purchase white rabbit and dye it any shade you desire using tintex for small dye lots. Color possibilities are almost infinite—try it. Fur dubbed flies can be left shaggy and fuzzy. This adds the extra dimension of translucence which is a definite advantage to any fly, but is especially effective on nymphs.

DRY

The most difficult to tie is the dry fly, which is also the most fun to use. A good day of dry fly fishing is not easily forgotten; these are the memories that linger. Dry flies float on the surface of the water and resemble insects that come to the surface to hatch, mayflies being the most common type. Use only the best possible available materials to tie the dry fly. Our dry fly will be the Light Cahill.

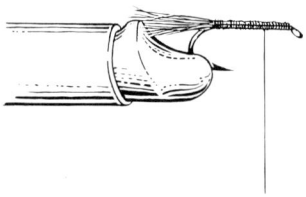

1. Attach light ginger hackle barbules for the tail. Tie in full length of shank of hook for durability.

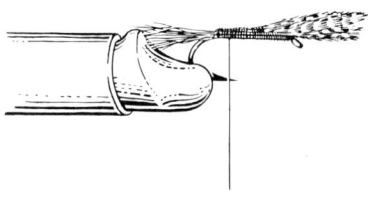

2. Next attach woodduck wings, tie wing butts into full length of body, taper with scissors.

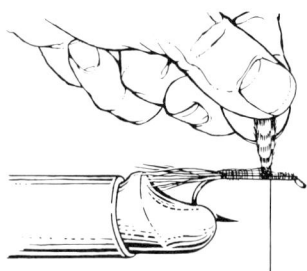

3. Pull wings into upright position with left hand, put several turns in front of wings, divide with figure eight knots, secure firmly with thread.

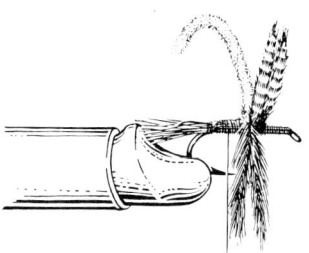

4. Attach two hackles (one for sparse fly) to the rear of divided cocked wings, tie hackle butts into body (whole length of body). This secures hackel butts.

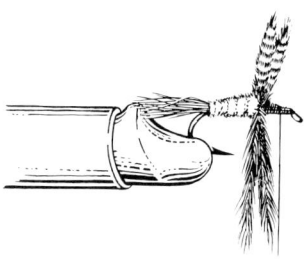

5. Spin fox fur body, wrap and taper slightly. This makes for a neat fly that will float better.

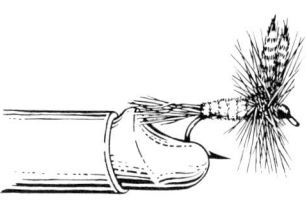

6. Now wind hackles, one to the rear of wings and one in front of wings and we have the Light Cahill.

HINTS: Wings and hackles have always been most difficult. By attaching hackles and wings as the second step, we have been able to secure each and have plenty of room to wind hackles as last step. Hair wings and all types of flies can be tied in this manner. Ray Bergman describes this way back in the 1930's so this method is not new, but has never been described and photographed as here.

BASS BUGS

Clipped deer hair bass bugs are really great sport on the fly rod. This is a slow, messy operation but you can really save money by tying your own bass bugs. You must use *deer body hair*, not bucktails, for bugs. Deer body hair is hollow and will spin properly to cover the shank of the hook. We will tie Tap Tappley's Red Head Bass Bug.

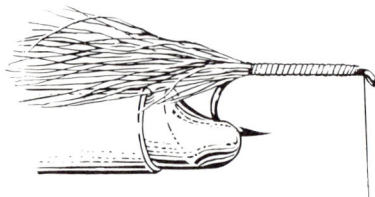

1. Attach hook, tie in white bucktail for tail, leave long as in photograph. Use monocord for thread.

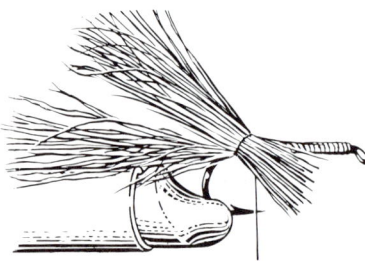

2. Using white hollow deer body hair, place a bunch about the diameter of a pencil on the shank. First turn is light to hold the hair in place. Second turn is as hard as possible without breaking the thread. This will cause hair to flair out in all directions. Add bunches of white deer body to form first half of the fly.

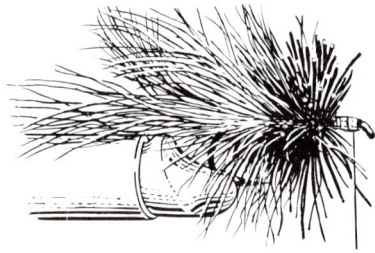

3. Second half of body is red deer body hair. This has been dyed. Now your bug will look like the fuzzy conglomeration pictured in photograph 3. For size 1/0 or 2 it will take twelve to eighteen bunches each the size of a pencil diameter.

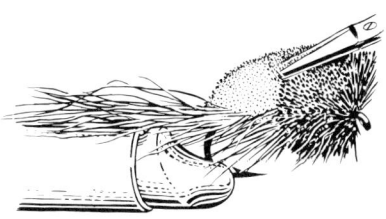

4. Begin to trim and shape the body with scissors, clipping a little at a time. It is easier to take fly out of vise to trim and cut the body hair. This gives a good look at the whole body at one time. Don't trim too much at a time.

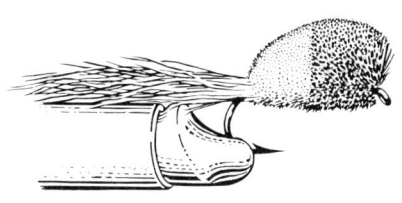

5. The completed bass bug. Many colors of dyed deer body hair are available so you can get just about any color you wish. You can make very fancy and elaborate bugs by using legs, antennae and your own ideas. Each false cast will dry the bug out.

HINTS: Muddler minnow heads, Irresistible bodies, Rat Face MacDougals bodies are all made in the same manner by attaching the deer body hair and trimming and shaping with scissors. The clipped deer hair body fly is probably the best floating fly ever invented. It is also very durable if tied on tightly. Don't be afraid to put as much pressure as possible on the body hair to make it flair up and out. This is the secret of a good tight body. Push the hair to the rear of the hook to get the hair on as tightly as possible. You will make mistakes on your first attempts. By practice, your flies will show improvement. Keep on trying and you have to end up with a better fly.

ATLANTIC SALMON HAIRWING

Salmon hairwing flies are strictly American in origin, very easy to tie and excellent for taking salmon. We will tie the Ingall's Butterfly.

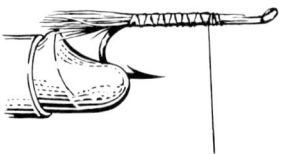

1. Attach red tail, red hackle fibers.

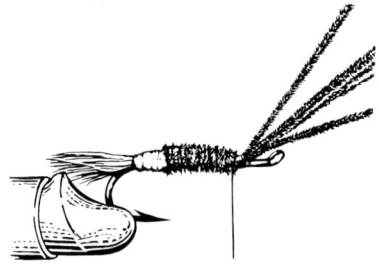

2. Attach green wool butt and peacock herl body.

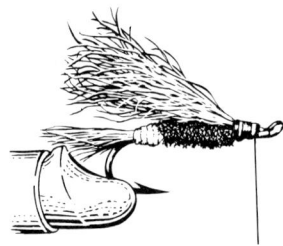

3. Attach white impali wing material.

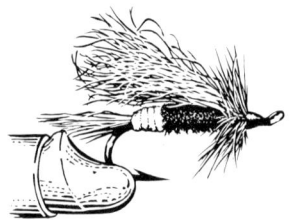

4. Place brown hackle in place and wind on.

JIGS

Many species of fresh water and salt water fish can be taken on a jig. A jig is a special hook style imbedded in a lead form or head. The lead gives the lure the added weight so it can be cast easily. It is usually used in spin fishing. The lure is worked in a series of jerks and pumps while being retrieved causing the lure to dart and move erratically. This makes the lure most enticing.

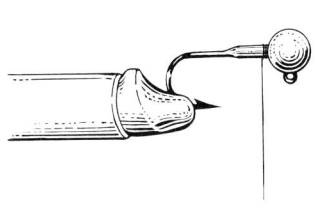

1. Attach thread at forward part of lead body.

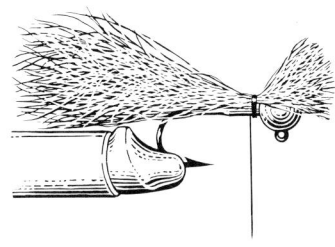

2. Attach a good size bunch of white bucktail on top of lead body.

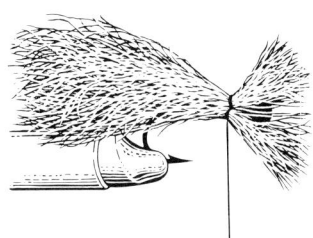

3. Attach a similar bunch of bucktail on under part of lead head body.

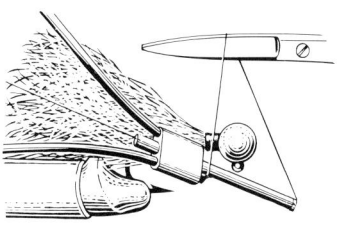

4. Wrap head with half hitches.

5. Paint lead head yellow, red, blue, etc., with colored lacquer.

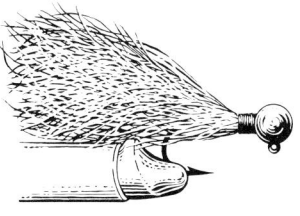

6. Completed jig with painted lead head.

DEFINITION OF FLY TYING TERMS

ABDOMEN—rear body portion of nymphs

BARBLESS—a style of hook with no barb

BARBULES—individual fibers of feathers, used as tails

BASS BUG—fly style made from deer body hair

BIVISIBLE—dry fly with hackle in place of body

BOBBIN—thread holder used in fly tying operations

BODKIN—sharp pointed tool for applying glue, etc.

BODY—portion of the fly between tail and head

BUCKTAIL—subsurface fly to resemble baitfish or attractor; wing usually made of bucktail

BUTT—a winding of herl at rear of body

CHEEK—portion of streamer fly to resemble gills, usually made from silver pheasant

CHENILLE—round fuzzy cotton material on cotton cord

COLLAR—hackle tied back slightly on wet and bucktails

COVERT—top covering of thorax on nymphs

DIVIDED WING—separation of wing materials to resemble mayfly style wings as on mayfly

DRY FLY—a fly tied to float on surface, usually tied to resemble a specific mayfly

FAN WING—a style of dry fly, usually made from woodduck white fans (or breast feathers)

FEATHER—basic material for many flies. Feathers from most birds are usable. Some species of birds are protected, jungle cock for example.

FLY—artificial copy of natural fly by tying furs, feathers, silks, etc. on a hook

GRIZZLY—black and white hackles from a Plymouth Rock rooster, rare and expensive

HACKLE—small feathers from a rooster neck used as part of a dry and wet fly at front of fly

HACKLE PLIERS—tool used to attach hackles on flies

HAIR—bucktails, squirrel tails, etc. used as wings

HEAD—last step in tying of fly, thread is tapered to secure the fly firmly in place

HOOK BARB—cut portion near point to hold fish

HOOK BEND—rounded portion at rear of hook

HOOK EYE—rounded front portion of hook, used to attach leader to fly

HOOK FINISH—most fresh water hooks are bronzed, black hooks are jappaned and are rust resistant. Salt water hooks are Z Nickel, tinned or stainless

HOOK GAPE—space between the point and shank of hook

HOOK POINT—sharp end of hook, to penetrate fish

HORNS—single pair of feather section over topping

IMPALI—tail from young calf, sometimes called kip

JAPANNED HOOK—hook finish in blue black enamel, usually used in Atlantic salmon flies

JIGS—large hooks with lead heads and bucktail tails

JUNGLE COCK—bird from India, now protected. Eyes are used in flies, only synthetics now available

LACQUER—used to protect the head of fly, clear or black

LIMMERICK—a parabolic shaped hook, usually nymph streamer or bucktail style hook

MALLARD—white and black breast feathers or wings

MARIBOU—soft, white breast feathers from storks

MODEL PERFECT—style of hook with round bend

MUSKRAT—gray underfur most used as body material

NYMPH—style of subsurface fly, imitates one of the stages of natural insects

NYLON—synthetic to take the place of silk, furs, etc.

PALMER HACKLE—dry fly with hackle in place of body

PARACHUTE—dry fly with hackles tied on top of fly

PEACOCK HERL—strands of metallic, bronze peacock. Very useful as a body material for wets, drys, etc.

PEACOCK EYE—strands from peacock eye, excellent quills

PEACOCK SWORD—usually used for tails or topping

QUILLS—primary and secondary wing feathers make excellent wing quills. Stripped peacock eyes and quills stripped from saddles make excellent bodies for flies

RABBIT—basic soft fur for dubbing, easily dyed

RIBBING—spiral windings over the body

SADDLE HACKLE—long feathers from rear of top of rooster

SHANK—portion of hook between eye and bend

SHOULDER—area on fly on both sides behind head

SILK—useful body material for all flies

SPROAT BEND—slightly parabolic bend, usually used on wet fly type hooks

SPUN FUR—a method of placing fur on bodies of flies

STREAMER—a style of subsurface fly to resemble baitfish or tied as colorful attractor flies

TAG—winding of silk, tinsel, etc. at rear of body

TERRESTRIAL—a style of fly to imitate land insects

THREAD—usually silk or nylon, 2/0 heavy, 4/0 medium, 6/0 fine

THROAT—tied under head of fly, sometimes called beard and can be tied collar style

TINSEL—metallic material used for bodies and rib

THORAX—front third portion of nymph style fly

TIP—a winding of floss or tinsel behind the body

TOPPING—materials tied over the wing as topping

VISE—basic tool to hold flies while tying fly

VIKING—hook style, combination of model perfect and sproat, usually a dry fly hook

WET FLY—a style of fly to be used sub-surface

ESSENTIAL TOOLS AND MATERIALS

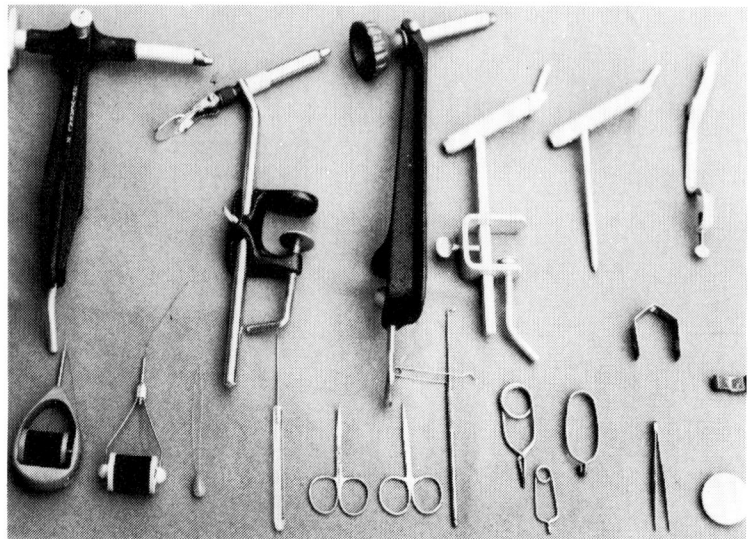

1 - Universal II Vise (Rotary); 2 - Thompson Model A Vise; 3 - Thompson Model B Vise; 4 - Universal Stationary Vise; 5 - Universal Streamside Vise; 6 - Thompson H Vise; 7 - Bobbins; 8 - Bobbin Threader; 9 - Bodkin; 10 - Scissors; 11 - Whip Finish; 12 - Hackle Pliers; 13 - Material Bobbin; 14 - Material Clip; 15 - Tweezers; 16 - Wax.

17 - Dry Fly Necks; 18 - Red Squirrel; 19 - Goose Quills; 20 - Gray Squirrel; 21 - Bucktail; 22 - Floss; 23 - Hooks; 24 - Duck Quills; 25 - Saddle Hackle; 26 - Dry Fly Hackle; 27 - Wool, Chenille; 28 - Tinsel; 29 - Furs; 30 - Calftail (Impali).

BLACK NOSE DACE

HISTORY AND ORIGIN

In 1947, "Art Flick's Streamside Guide" listed only one bucktail, the Black Nose Dace, which really copies many various types of small fish. This fly will resemble chubs, dace and a host of small minnows that have the dark lateral line down their side. Larger sizes are a good early season choice, sizes 4 and 6 to be specific, and as the water drops, sizes 8, 10 and 12 become effective. A very good fly if fished in the holding pockets or down deep. If you can spot a large fish that is chasing minnows, drop it in front of him to distract him, and you may entice the fish.

DRESSING

HOOK—Mustad #3665A, #9575 or #38941
SIZES—4-6-8-10-12
THREAD—Black-silk, monocord or nylon
TAG—Red yarn, very short
BODY—Flat silver tinsel
WING—LOWER THIRD—Polar bear or white impali
       MIDDLE THIRD—Black skunk or black bear
       TOP THIRD—Brown bucktail

LITTLE BROOK TROUT

HISTORY AND ORIGIN

This fly is of fairly recent origin, having been first tied by Sam Slaymaker of Pennsylvania in the late 1950's, there were other Little Trout in this series. Leaning more on the side of exact imitation, this fly tries to very closely copy the natural color and basic color tones of little trout that on occasion provide a tasty morsel for larger trout. A durable fly as all bucktails when tied properly, this fly can be a very consistent taker of large fish on the prowl. Tied on a small hook it is a very good fry imitation.

DRESSING

HOOK—Mustad #3665A, #9575
SIZES—2-4-6-8-10-12
THREAD—Black-silk, monocord or nylon
TAIL—Sparse bright green bucktail, over which is tied
    bright red floss
BODY—Cream spun fur
RIBBING—Flat silver tinsel
THROAT—Sparse orange bucktail, long
WING—Bottom Layer—Sparse white bucktail
          Second Layer—Sparse orange bucktail
          Third Layer—Sparse green bucktail
          Top Layer—Sparse barred badger hair

MICKEY FINN

HISTORY AND ORIGIN

The flash of red and yellow spiced with the glitter of tinsel sure does make an attractive combination. Probably the bucktail that all anglers know, a very simple fly, good for the beginner to cut teeth on. This fly is originally from Canada and was made popular by John Alden Knight, of Solunar Tables fame in the 1930's. A very durable fly that will take trout, salmon, bass and just about any thing that swims. Can also be tied as a feather streamer, maribou, and a married wet fly: certainly as versatile as any fly ever tied on a hook.

DRESSING

HOOK—Mustad #3665A, #9575 or #38941
SIZES—2-4-6-8-10-12 or tandem 2 and 4
BODY—Flat silver tinsel
RIBBING—Oval silver tinsel
WING—Bottom Layer, Yellow bucktail
        Middle Layer, Red bucktail
        Top Layer, Yellow bucktail
THREAD—Black-silk, monocord or nylon

LIGHT EDSON TIGER

HISTORY AND ORIGIN

Bill Edson, another Maine fly tyer, evolved this fly in 1929; long shanked hooks are preferred in this pattern. The pattern below is the more accepted one today, differing very little from the original. Yellow is always a good color and especially yellow bucktail, which tied sparse will breathe and pulsate slightly. The peacock body will give off an orange appearance under the water, and the action of the peacock fibers holds great appeal. A great trout fly all over the world, even in such remote places as Labrador and Ungava.

DRESSING

HOOK—Mustad #3665A, #3907B
SIZES—4-6-8-10
THREAD—Yellow and lacquered yellow
TAG—Flat gold tinsel
TAIL—Barred wood duck as in photo
BODY—Peacock herl, tied full
WING—Yellow bucktail, tied shorter than usual
TOPPING—Two red hackles, tied very short
CHEEKS—Jungle cock, tied short

WARDEN'S WORRY

HISTORY AND ORIGIN

Early in the 1930's, Warden Joseph Stickney designed and originated this pattern, a very aptly named fly which is excellent for fishing deep with a sinking line on the bottom, and a good copy of many kinds of food. Basic coloration can represent large nymphs, and other forms of food on the bottom. Tie this fly as indicated in the dressing below and you will have one of the most universally accepted bucktails and the fly will catch trout and salmon quite readily, especially early in the season as the water first begins to warm up.

DRESSING

HOOK—Mustad #3665A, #9575 or #38941
THREAD—Black-silk, monocord or nylon
TAG—Flat gold tinsel
TAIL—Two pieces red goose, sweeping up, long
BODY—Fairly full, yellow orange wool, tied fuzzy by pick-
    ing out with bodkin
RIBBING—Narrow gold tinsel, oval
THROAT—Collar style, yellow hackle
WING—Sparsely dressed, light brown bucktail

HARRIS SPECIAL

HISTORY AND ORIGIN

This is a fairly local pattern popular in New Hampshire especially in northern areas where it was first tied by Oliver G. Harris of Warner, N.H. in 1931. The son of the originator is now a tackle salesman and provided the following notes: Fly was not widely used until 1960's when Lonnie Harris and his brother sold the fly to commercial outlets all over New England. This is typical of small brightly colored flies to take brookies. This type of fly is particularly effective on ponds, dredged on the bottom with a sinking line. Vary the retrieve working the fly slowly, then a jerky movement and lastly as fast as you can make the fly move. This fly is a really good fly for wild native brookies. This is also a good pattern for fall fishing on those crisp, clear, autumn mornings.

DRESSING

HOOK—Mustad #3665A, #9575, #38941
SIZE—6-8-10-12-14
THREAD—Black silk or nylon
TAIL—Golden pheasant crests (or tippets)
BODY—Flat silver tinsel, double wrapped
THROAT—Wisps of red bucktail, long and sparse
WING—Sparse white bucktail, veiled with lemon wood-
    duck

MISS SHARON

HISTORY AND ORIGIN

Sebago Lake in Maine has the fame as being the "Home of Salmo Sebago," the site where the landlock salmon was first identified and classified. Many good tyers have tied flies for the area. One of them is Arthur Libby of Standish, Maine, who originated the Miss Sharon in 1972.

In the beginning of the season the fly can be slightly more full, but as the season progresses, it should become increasingly sparse. One of the theories advocated is that the salmon cannot see quite as well in the early season because of roily water and a slight ocular deficiency from poor feeding under the ice all winter. As the season progresses and feeding is more available, the eyesight is restored, the water clears, and the salmon becomes more selective, an interesting theory.

They go to the extreme effort of counting each and every strand of bucktail that goes into making up the mixed wing of the Miss Sharon.

DRESSING

HOOK—Front Mustad #3906, size 4 Rear Mustad, treble, size 10
TANDEM CONNECTOR—50-pound nylon
BODY—Silver flat embossed tinsel
WING—Mixed four layers of bucktail
      First—White bucktail, sparse
      Second—fluorescent orange bucktail, sparse
      Third—Red bucktail, sparse
      Fourth—Black bucktail, sparse

LLAMA

HISTORY AND ORIGIN

Ray Benedict of Wisconsin first introduced the Llama to Eric Leiser, who has popularized the fly pattern to the fly tying public. The wing is made from a woodchuck's body; try to obtain a spring- or fall-kill woodchuck. Chucks taken during the summer are sparse and the fur is not as suitable. The hair is fawn-colored at the base and turns to dark chocolate brown that ends with a golden ginger tip. Actually, many fly tyers are ignoring a great supply of excellent domestic materials such as woodchuck, red fox, muskrat, beaver, and several other native American animal furs that are plentiful.

Our pattern differs slightly in that we include the golden ginger underfur as part of the wing. This gives the wing a two-tone effect which is striking in color and more full. Woodchuck can be used as wing material for traditional Atlantic salmon flies such as the Rusty Rat, Silver Rat, and several others.

DRESSING

HOOK—Mustad #38941
SIZES—6-8-10-12-14
THREAD—Black pre-waxed nylon
BODY—Red floss, oval and papered
RIBBING—Gold oval tinsel
WING—Guard hairs with golden ginger underfur from
      woodchuck
COLLAR—Grizzly hackle, tied collar style.

MAYNARD'S MARVEL

HISTORY AND ORIGIN

A colorful effective fly, especially on upcountry ponds and streams when dredged along the bottom with a sinking line. This is a fly from the Pittsburg, N.H. area, a local guide whose last name was Maynard originated this pattern in the late 20's, first brought to the N. Conway area in 1931 by Carl Stilphen, a local florist.

A very popular fly in N.H., it has many variations, one is a fly with all golden pheasant wing as used on Lake Winnipesaukee for trolling, I feel the dressing is more in keeping with the original as listed below.

DRESSING

HOOK—Mustad #38941 or #9671
SIZE—8-10-12-14
TAIL—Red hackle barbules
BODY—Silver tinsel, flat embossed medium
THROAT—Red hackle barbules
WING—Bottom layer—golden pheasant
      Middle layer—light blue impali
      Top layer—mallard flank, sheathed.

GRAY GHOST

HISTORY AND ORIGIN

One of Maine's most popular flies, first tied by Mrs. Carrie Stevens of Upper Dam, Maine. Her husband Wallace was a guide in the area of Rangeley, first fished in 1924, it took a brookie of 7 pounds and second place in the *Field & Stream* contest. Tied to resemble a smelt, which is a primary source of food for trout and salmon. Mrs. Stevens also tied other patterns, the Black Ghost, Wizard, etc. Her trademark was a red band in the middle of the head of the fly. Probably the most sought after early season fly in the Northern New England states.

DRESSING

HOOK—Mustad #9575, #3665A or #94720
SIZE—2-4-6-8-10 or Tandem Troller 2 and 4
HEAD—Black with a red band
TAG—Narrow flat silver tinsel
BODY—Orange silk thinly dressed
RIBBING—Flat narrow silver tinsel
THROAT—Four or five strands of peacock herl, small bunch of white bucktail beyond bend. A golden pheasant crest feather.
WING—A golden pheasant crest feather over which four grayish olive saddles are tied.
SHOULDERS—Silver pheasant cheeks, long and full
CHEEKS—Jungle Cock

BLACK GHOST

HISTORY AND ORIGIN

A famous taxidermist of Oquossoc, Maine, Herb Welch, who fished Mooselookmeguntic with one of our presidents, invented this fly in 1927. Currently a well-known fly all over the world where salmonoid species are caught. The Percy Tackle Company of Portland, Maine sold thousands of this pattern from the 1930's until just recently.

A lady tyer, Nellie Newton, did a great deal of tying of this pattern in the late 20's and later, it was used and tied by a great many tyers and is still a favorite fly of anglers.

DRESSING

HOOK—Mustad #9575, #3665A, or #94720
SIZE—4-6-8-10 or Tandem Troller 2 & 4
THREAD—black silk or monocord
TAIL—Sparsely tied yellow hackle fibers
BODY—Tapered at both ends, full in the middle, black silk
RIBBING—Flat silver tinsel, medium
THROAT—Sparsely tied yellow hackle fibers
WING—Four white saddle hackles
CHEEKS—Jungle cock

NINE THREE

HISTORY AND ORIGIN

The originator caught a salmon of nine pounds, three ounces the first day the fly was used, hence the name. Dr. Hubert Sanborn of Waterville, Maine caught this fine salmon on Messalonskee Lake, Maine in 1936. The original pattern has the green saddles tied on flat, rather than on edge as usually seen on the flies available today. The Nine Three looks odd, but a very good fly to cast or troll, a fine choice for right after "ice out" conditions of the spring in the lakes of the North New England area where trolling for landlocked salmon is so popular.

DRESSING

HOOK—Mustad #9575, #3665A or #94720
SIZES—2-4-6-8-10 and Tandem Troller 2-4
THREAD—Black-silk, monocord or nylon
BODY—Flat silver tinsel
WING—Sparse white bucktail, tied beyond the bend of the hook. Over the bucktail place three green saddle hackles, tied flat. Tie three black saddles upright.
CHEEKS—Jungle cock

GOLDEN DARTER

HISTORY AND ORIGIN

A fairly recent fly pattern, this fly tries to imitate the more common type of forage fish that abounds in most aquatic areas. Carefully developed by Lew Oatman in New York State in the early 1950's, this is an early forerunner of the type of fly that closely resembles food forms. By carefully selecting materials and putting them together in a precise manner the end result is a close copy. This fly can easily be taken for many types of forage fish that abound in many areas, can also be used as a locator fly.

DRESSING

HOOK—Mustad #9575, #3665A
SIZES—4-6-8-10-12
THREAD—Black-silk, monocord or nylon
TAIL—Mottled turkey
TAG—Four turns of gold tinsel
BODY—Tapered yellowish gold floss
RIBBING—Flat gold tinsel
THROAT—Tip of one jungle cock body feather
WING—Golden edged badger saddles, four
CHEEKS—Jungle cock

BALLOU SPECIAL

HISTORY AND ORIGIN

The landlocked salmon or "poor man's" salmon are readily accessible in the early cold days of April. The originator of the maribou style of fly was A. I. Ballou of Litchfield, Maine who tied creations all winter to copy the smelt, the main food of the salmon as they follow the smelt run up the rivers on the spawning run. He felt that the maribou material with a dark topping of peacock herl best imitated a smelt and was a most effective fly. This pattern was first tied in 1921 and is not as popular as it once was during the 20's and 30's. However the material maribou is now one of the most used materials for streamer wings and streamer flies. This fly tied in smaller sizes is a very good pattern for stream or river fishing for trout and salmon, especially skittered across the rapid runs.

DRESSING

HOOK—Mustad #9575 or #3665A
SIZE—4-6-8-10-12
THREAD—Black nylon or silk
TAIL—One or two golden pheasant crest feathers curving downward
BODY—Medium flat silver tinsel
UNDERWING—Red bucktail, slightly long
OVERWING—Maribou tied full and over red bucktail
TOPPING—Peacock herl about 12 strands to give dark top outline
CHEEKS—Jungle cock

GOLDEN DEMON

HISTORY AND ORIGIN

The Golden Demon is probably the most used fly on Back Lake and in the Connecticut Lakes area of N.H. This fly has an interesting and well - traveled background. The fly was originated in England and brought to New Zealand where Zane Grey used it in the 1920's. He then brought some flies back to the West Coast for steelhead and salmon. Then the fly appeared on the salmon rivers of New Brunswick, especially on the Cains River. From New Brunswick the pattern filtered down to the area of northern New Hampshire in the early 1930's and has been a most popular pattern in that area ever since. The orange throat is supposed to be the color that is repulsive to demons and is tied in several variations such as the Silver Demon and Black Demon.

DRESSING

HOOK—Mustad #3665A or #9575
SIZE—4-6-8-10-12
THREAD—Black pre-waxed nylon
TAIL—Golden pheasant crest
BODY—Golden yellow wool
RIBBING—Gold flat tinsel
THROAT—Hot orange hackle
WING—Bronze mallard

CARDINELLE

HISTORY AND ORIGIN

Bill Chiba of Springfield, Mass., showed this fly to Paul Kukkonen of Worcester, Mass., in late 1960's. Paul popularized the pattern by use of his films on fishing and hunting to more than 25,000 anglers and hunters per year. Paul changed the pattern as listed below, noting "I have taken all species of trout, landlocks, Atlantic salmon, small mouth bass, large mouth bass, walleye, pike, stripers, blues and coho. This fly took a 5 pound 9 ounce brookie in Maine. I now must consider it in the top 5 streamers. I hear of many new flies every year, 99% of them are failures. This one clicked." This is a very popular pattern in southern New England.

DRESSING

HOOK—Mustad #3665A or #9575, 4x, 5x or 6x long
THREAD—Hot Orange
BODY—Fluorescent orange or fluorescent red wool body
UNDERWING—Fluorescent nylon hair, orange or red
WING—Cerise maribou
HACKLE—Yellow saddles, tied back collar style and long
NOTE—This fly has no tail or ribbing.

BINGHAM SPECIAL

HISTORY AND ORIGIN

The originator of this small casting streamer is Bob Bedell of Solon, Maine, one of the old-timer Maine Down East fly tyers. Its small size is especially easy to cast to landlocks, brookies, and rainbows of the Bingham area of Maine.

First used in 1972 with a sinking line and dredging down deep style of fishing for the cold-water species of fish that live in that area. The early season has tough conditions; the fish tend to be logy and down deep and you have to get down to them with sinking lines and flies. This fly is particularly effective in Carry Pond in the Bingham area.

This bait-type fly can be made with materials which are plentiful and easy to use. The state of Maine has to be considered the bucktail/streamer capital of the world. The smelt fly patterns alone would keep you tying for a very long cold winter.

DRESSING

HOOK—Mustad #9575
SIZES—10-12
THREAD—Black pre-waxed nylon
BODY—Flat silver tinsel
THROAT—Long as hook, white impali
        Peacock herl tied directly under hook
WING—Underwing of yellow impali, tied length of hook
      Topwing—four grizzly saddles, usual streamer
           style
CHEEKS—Brown breast of partridge
EYES—White with black center, clear lacquer over

WINNIPESAUKEE SMELT

HISTORY AND ORIGIN

This fly was invented by Jim Warner of Wolfboro, New Hampshire, one of the best streamer and tandem fly tyers in the Northeast. Jim states the following: This fly was originated in 1957 to imitate the local smelt of Lake Winnipesaukee. I have felt that the bucktail was needed for the body of the wing to keep that flimsy little marabou feather from turning under the hook. Of course the peacock herl gives it the look of the lateral line. It is very important that it be stressed that the white marabou feather should have the smallest possible quill so that the fly has the greatest action. The tipping of Silver Pheasant Crest is sometimes substituted with Ostrich Herl. I prefer the eyes with a 'bulging look' which I build up with thick pearlescent lacquer."

DRESSING

HOOK—Any 6XL to 8XL long, size 2-4-6 or tandem.
THREAD—Black nylon 4/0
BODY—Flat silver tinsel, double-wrapped.
WING—First layer—Sparse white bucktail
        Second layer—3 or 4 thin strands of peacock herl
        Third layer—Sparse dyed orchid bucktail
        Fourth layer—A single white marabou feather (one must be carefully selected to have little or no quill)
        Top layer—2 or 3 natural blue-black silver pheasant crests, curving down over the wing and nearly the same length if possible.
HEAD—Pearlescent lacquer with black pupil

COACHMAN

HISTORY AND ORIGIN

Tom Bosworth, the Coachman of George IV, William IV and Queen Victoria for the royal family of England was the originator of this fly in the 1830's. The coachman was also a fly dresser and superb angler, who could take a pipe out of a surprised pedestrian's mouth with a whip from a moving coach. We now have the Royal Coachman, Leadwing Coachman, Fan Wing Royal Coachman, and other variations of the Coachman fly. The peacock body does make for an unexcelled body material which is readily available and very easy to use.

DRESSING

HOOK—Mustad #3906, and #3906B
SIZES—6-8-10-12-14-16
THREAD—Black-silk, waxed nylon, or monocord
TAG—Gold flat tinsel
BODY—Bronze peacock herl, tied full (fine gold wire may be wound as ribbing over herl for added durability)
HACKLE—Coachman brown, collar style
WINGS—White duck quill

SILVER DOCTOR

HISTORY AND ORIGIN

During the 1860's and 1870's, fly tyers were working on patterns to attract trout and salmon to the creel. Bright, colorful flies seemed to be extremely productive on wild fish and the same holds true today. James Wight, P. S. Wilkinson and other early tyers worked on variations of this pattern. The married wings of flies like the Silver Doctor are the classic style of tying flies for trout and salmon. The proportion and styling of this fly makes a very outstanding fly. It takes good materials, patience and some degree of skill to produce this artificial fly.

DRESSING

HOOK—Mustad #3906 or #3906B
SIZES—6-8-10-12-14
THREAD—Black silk, monocord or nylon
TAIL—Golden pheasant tippets
BODY—Flat silver tinsel
THROAT—Silver Doctor blue
WING—Four married layers, from top to bottom
    Mottled turkey quill
    Silver Doctor Blue goose quill
    Scarlet goose quill
    Yellow goose quill

PARMACHEENE BELLE

HISTORY AND ORIGIN

Parmacheene Lake in the Rangeley area of western Maine lends its name to this fly, originated by Henry P. Wells in 1878, who also wrote "Fly Rods and Fly Tackle" in 1885. A gaudy and brilliantly colored fly, it is still widely used in the far north of New England and Canada where wild trout still abound. The basic coloration is that of a fin of a brook trout which was sometimes used as bait. The married wings are a thing of beauty and the fly is still a killer fly where wild native trout will respond with energy readily to this bright fly.

DRESSING

HOOK—Mustad #3906
SIZES—6-8-10-12-14
THREAD—Black-silk, monocord or nylon
TAIL—Red and white hackle barbules, mixed
BODY—Yellow silk floss
RIBBING—Gold tinsel, flat
THROAT—Red and white hackle barbules, mixed
WINGS—Married, red on top, one quarter. White on bottom, three quarters

PROFESSOR

HISTORY AND ORIGIN

A professor of Edinburg University, under the pen name of Christopher North designed this fly in the early 1800's. His real name was John Wilson, 1785-1854. Supposedly the fly came into being in the following way: The professor was out of flies and using a yellow buttercup for a body and a few threads from a sock, he fashioned a yellow bodied fly that took trout. Later the fly was refined and a few materials added for effect. The buttercup yellow body is still with us today 175 years later and still quite a popular fly.

DRESSING

HOOK—Mustad #3906
SIZES—6-8-10-12-14
THREAD—Black-silk, monocord or nylon
TAIL—Red hackle barbules
BODY—Buttercup yellow silk floss
RIBBING—Gold flat tinsel
THROAT—Brown hackle barbules
WING—Mallard flank

HARE'S EAR

HISTORY AND ORIGIN

This old pattern was in existence prior to 1839, when T. C. Hofland referred to the fur from between the ears of a hare. The originator can not be traced, but is from England, brought by the settlers to use on American waters. A sombre pattern, it forms the basis of many imitations of natural trout foods. Not lavish or flashy, but still a fly that has accounted for many fish for a very long time, the gold tinsel gives the added spark every fly needs. This pattern seems to be even a more killing fly when worn and tattered, the light pattern may change slightly, making it more effective.

DRESSING

HOOK—Mustad #3906
SIZES—6-8-10-12-14-16
THREAD—Black-silk, monocord or nylon
TAIL—Brown hackle fibers
BODY—Hare's ear dubbing, ribbed with flat gold tinsel
HACKLE—Picked out at the throat to represent legs
WINGS—Mallard wing quill section

IRON BLUE WINGLESS

HISTORY AND ORIGIN

Soft hackle flies are now back in style, and for many oldtimers the flies were never out of style. This fly is most deadly just fished under the surface film to imitate a struggling nymph that is just about to hatch. We have experienced some very fine angling for brown trout on the local rivers using this pattern on dark cloudy days. By utilizing the soft hackle we get a breathing effect on the fly as it is worked through the water. This very closely resembles a natural insect in its natural environment. This pattern was evolved by James Leisenring and the book "The Art of Tying the Wet Fly" is the bible for wet fly fishing and flies. Leisenring was a perfectionist in the flies he tied and the patterns are excellent. An angler could use nothing but this series of flies and be a top rod anywhere.

DRESSING

HOOK—Mustad #94840 or #3906
SIZE—12-14-16-18
THREAD—Crimson or scarlet silk or nylon
TAIL—Short honey dun hackle fibers
BODY—Dark mole or muskrat fur dubbed on crimson
    silk, very thin at tail to expose silk
RIBBING—Fine gold wire
HACKLE—Honey dun hackle

YELLOW DUN

HISTORY AND ORIGIN

In many instances one of the best methods to land the wary old *Salmo fario* or brown trout is after-dark angling with a large wet fly. With the cover of darkness, the brown is not as wary as during the daylight. During the years between 1920 to 1940 a famous hole the Goodsell Hole, at the junction of the Allegheny River and Mill Creek in Pennsylvania yielded many fine browns that were on their way to spawning grounds. These fish would lay over for a spell at this pool. An angling dentist, Doc Phillips, had a very fine fly tyer in his wife and she was the originator of this pattern in the 1920's. The secret was in the body of the fly and the exact ingredients were never spelled out. The body was of a pinkish hue when dry and sort of bloody red when wet. You can experiment with this one.

DRESSING

HOOK—Mustad #3906
SIZES—4-6-8-10
THREAD—Black nylon
TAIL—Black and white barred wood duck
BODY—Fleshy pink fur dubbing; could be dyed mohair, should be bloody red when wet
HACKLE—Dark ginger, collar style
WING—Lemon wood duck

OLIVE HERON

HISTORY AND ORIGIN

This pattern was developed and tied by one of the best fly tyers and anglers in New Hampshire, Nick Lambrou of Manchester, in 1972. Tied especially to be used for land-locked salmon as a shrimp fly copy during the early season angling in the Lake Winnipesaukee area. The fly when tied in various sizes imitates some lake and stream minnows. Best usage of the fly is with a floating line and fine long leaders to coax fussy and uncooperative land-locks into striking as the fly is constantly cast and floated over the holding fish.

Variations of the pattern can be gray, black, brown, etc. Keep the same style palmer hackle and the wing format; change the base colors only in the fly. When used in rivers, streams, and ponds, it becomes a good fly for all species of trout.

For some strange reason rainbow trout seem to like this fly style and dressing. The Olive Heron has also proved itself in the very limited sea run brown fishery of coastal New England. Give this fly a good workout; it is a real sleeper.

DRESSING

HOOK—Mustad #9671
THREAD—Olive pre-waxed nylon
SIZES—6-8-10-12
BODY—Olive dubbed seal
RIB—Olive palmered hackle, full
WING—Wood duck flank

LEISENRING BLACK GNAT

HISTORY AND ORIGIN

One of the indications of a well-tied fly is not overdressing or making the fly too full, this is a pitfall of most beginners. The proper sparseness will allow the fibers, furs, and materials to work or act more lifelike in the water. Insects have tremendous movement as they swim about in their environment.

Jim Leisenring, one of the best wet fly tyers of all time, was a master in selection of the proper materials for tying his overall sparse but effective flies. His time-consuming efforts show in his work as he did indeed have some excellent flies that were simple but yet very effective. The book "The Art of Tying the Wet Fly and Fishing the Flymph" by Leisenring and Vernon Hidy shows the patterns, materials, and painstaking efforts to secure just the right material for each and every fly.

Black is a predominant color in many aquatic insects; at least, many are on the dark side and black is a very visible color in any trout stomach analysis.

DRESSING

HOOK—Mustad #3906
SIZES—12-14-16-18
THREAD—Crimson or claret silk
BODY—Black silk or two or three fibers from a crow's secondary wing feather
WINGS—Dark starling (optional)
HACKLE—Purplish black feather from the shoulder of a cock starling

TROUT FIN

HISTORY AND ORIGIN

There are times when a very bright, wild, gaudy pattern is irresistible to wild native "squaretails" in the northeast part of New England and eastern Canada. Long before artificial flies were available an old trick was to use the cut-off fins of the brookie for bait to attract their attention. As time wore on, the angler began to use flies and a duplicate of the trout fins was tied to resemble the real thing in furs, feathers, and silks. Thus we can see the relationship between the natural trout fin and the formation of the artificial fly as we know it today.

This fly is also very popular in a streamer/bucktail type by the use of longer hooks and materials. Dyed bucktails or calftails make a very pretty and unusual combination of the art of fly tying and visual imagination of nature. Today the streamer/bucktail type is probably more popular than the original wet. We have chosen to show the original pattern, the wet style with the married wing.

DRESSING

HOOK—Mustad #3906
SIZES—8-10-12-14-16
THREAD—Pre-waxed black nylon
TAIL—Red duck quill
BODY—Flat silver tinsel with very fine oval silver rib
HACKLE—Light ginger, tied back collar style
WING—Three layers, married matched duck, goose, or
      swan.
      Top to bottom — white, black (thin), and red.

LEADWING COACHMAN

HISTORY AND ORIGIN

One of the flies that has been around for a long time is the Leadwing Coachman, which the colonists brought with them from England. The two base ingredients of peacock herl and the slate gray mallard wing quill are among the best and most versatile of materials. The small fuzzy particles that stick out from the stem of the herl really move and undulate in the water, most important in wet flies. Many nymphs take on a slate gray color in the folded up pad section of the upper thorax as they go through the process of hatching.

Although peacock herl is an excellent material for bodies, it does have the definite problem of being very fragile, certainly one of the most difficult to make secure and lasting. There are several ways to prevent this fragility. You can place a light layer of pliobond, vinyl, or head cement along the body, wrap your herl over this, and let it adhere for a solid body. Some tyers twist several strands together with a strand of pre-waxed monocord in the center or use the old method of twisting a very fine single strand of gold wire over the body as a ribbing going in the opposite direction.

DRESSING

HOOK—Mustad #3906
SIZES—8-10-12-14-16
THREAD—Pre-waxed nylon, black
TAG—Gold flat mylar
BODY—Peacock herl tied full
RIBBING—Very fine gold wire
HACKLE—Brown, collar style
WING—Slate gray mallard quill

MARCH BROWN

HISTORY AND ORIGIN

This nymph pattern is an adaptation of Preston Jennings'
March Brown from his fine book "A Book of Trout Flies,"
Derrydale 1935. The Stenonema vicarium is one of the
earliest flies to emerge in the Northeast and a valuable
early season pattern. Art Flick also worked out some
good patterns of March Browns. The original pattern is of
English origin and has been used for many years with
many variations and dressings; also an Atlantic salmon
pattern. A good fly to use in waters of Northeast U. S. A.
but also good wherever trout are found.

DRESSING

HOOK—Mustad #38941 or #9671
SIZES—10-12-14
THREAD—Orange silk
TAIL—Red game cock barbules
BODY—Red fox belly, mixed with sandy fur from hare's
    ear
COVERT—Mallard flank
LEGS—Red game cock

DARK MOSSBACK

HISTORY AND ORIGIN

Dan Bailey of Livingston, Montana, first tied this most lifelike and durable fly. This is a woven body using nylon floss strands that are woven over a pre-shaped rubber body and the fly is very hardy. The light bottom and dark top are very realistic and give the general impression of the insect. Some of the earlier patterns had woven horsehair and raffia bodies; the dressing below is much tougher. A very good fly for larger streams and rivers, also good for lake fishing. Excellent directions on weaving are in "Art of Weaving Hair Hackles for Trout Flies", by G. F. Grant.

DRESSING

HOOK—Mustad #9671
SIZES—4-6-8-10
THREAD—Black nylon
BODY—Pre-shaped by wool or rubber to shape
TAILS AND LEGS—Condor quill or goose barbule dyed brown
WOVEN BODY—Weave so that a dark top and light yellow bottom is obtained

ATHERTON DARK NYMPH

HISTORY AND ORIGIN

John Atherton of Vermont originated this nymph in the early 1950's. His "The Fly and the Fish" is a very fine book and gives many solid thoughts about colors and fishing (an artist, he was very concerned about light patterns and translucency). His carefully selected materials and blending of the materials made outstanding flies. He also tried to simplify the selection of flies by tying careful imitations that have basic shades and color tones. His Atherton Light and Medium nymphs, along with the above pattern in all sizes would give an angler a very good selection of nymphs.

DRESSING

HOOK—Mustad #38941, #3906B
SIZES—8-10-12-14-16
THREAD—Red silk or monocord
TAIL—Sparse dark furnace barbules
BODY—Mixture of muskrat and dyed reddish brown
    seal, tied rough
RIB—Narrow gold oval tinsel
THORAX—Same as body
LEGS—Dark furnace, tied in near head
COVERT—Lacquered kingfisher

BLACK NYMPH

HISTORY AND ORIGIN

This fly is a basic fur dubbed fly of dyed beaver and dyed seal, the beaver gives the basic full shape and the seal the translucency that is so desirable. J. Edson Leonard in his fine book "Flies" says if he were to be limited to one material, it would be fur and I agree completely. By the wise use of dubbing furs, the fly tyer has almost endless possibilities to fashion flies. First tied in the early 1960's by the author, it is also tied in brown, gray, cream, olive and yellow in a wide range of sizes, this can cover any situations in the area of nymphs.

DRESSING

HOOK—Mustad #38941, #9671
SIZES—8-10-12-14
THREAD—Black pre-waxed nylon or monocord
TAIL—Sparse cock pheasant barbules
ABDOMEN—Mixture of ¾ dyed black beaver and ¼ dyed
    black seal
RIBBING—Fine oval gold, on abdomen only
LEGS—Black hackle, at base of covert
THORAX—As abdomen, tied full and fuzzy
COVERT—Mottled turkey

BIRD'S STONE FLY NYMPH NO. 2

HISTORY AND ORIGIN

In the late 1960's, Cal Bird, a fly tyer from California worked on this fur-dubbed fly. This fly is a nymph stage of a stone fly and by using the fur dubbing method, a finer body can be made by using fur as a raw material. The fur can be controlled to any shape and thickness and the blending process makes it easy to come up with any shade in the range of colors. Large nymphs like this are very popular out west and the eastern anglers would do well if they fished it on the bottom with a sinking line. Muskrat, possum, seal, beaver, fox are a few of the basic furs.

DRESSING

HOOK—Mustad #9671, #9672, #38941
SIZES—4-6-8-10
THREAD—Gray monocord
TAIL—Two gray goose fibers
ABDOMEN—Fur dubbed muskrat
THORAX—Peacock herl
COVERT—Clear plastic
LEGS—Blue dun hackle

GRAY MIDGE NYMPH

HISTORY AND ORIGIN

Ed Koch, in his "Fishing the Midge," 1972, tells of the effectiveness with minute copies of caddis nymphs. The waters of the LeTort and other spring creeks of Penna. abound in minute forms of insect life and as summer brings the streams low the wily brown becomes more difficult than ever to catch. The fly tyers of the Penna. area have done very much in the past 25 years to perfect the tying of very small flies to be used in the heat of mid-summer when many anglers used to quit, now we can have fishing all summer that will produce.

DRESSING

HOOKS—Mustad #94840, #94833, #94825
SIZES—16-18-20-22-24
THREAD—Gray nymph thread or waxed nylon
BODY—Muskrat fur, dubbed
HEAD—Peacock herl

CRANE FLY

HISTORY AND ORIGIN

Ernest Schwiebert has an excellent chapter in his book "Matching the Hatch" entitled, Lesser Trout Foods. This style of fly is from that source. There are many times that trout will not have a major type of predominant food and will have to settle for something that is readily available. The crane fly is one of these types. This fly can be fished on the bottom as you would any type of nymph or bottom food, slowly and smack dab on the bottom of the pond, lake or stream. There are many types of crane flies in North America and you may want to change the color format to your own regions, keep the same shape and form for the fly. The hook is bent at a slight curve as you first start to work on the fly. This gives the fly a nice shape. Do the bending with a pair of long-nose pliers first.

DRESSING

HOOK—Mustad #38941
SIZE—6-8-10-12
THREAD—Gray to match body
BODY—Three quarters light gray fur dubbing, one quarter dark gray fur dubbing
RIBBING—Fine oval gold ribbing
HORNS—Muskrat guard hairs

DAMSEL FLY

HISTORY AND ORIGIN

There are many colors and sizes of damsel flies. You may want to collect your own samples and types from your own local waters. Our pattern is one we evolved since 1970 and is similar in shape but the color is different. Basic colors are red-brown, olive, gray and orange. Again, this is primarily a pond or lake fly and can be a killer fly at certain times of the year. Best feeding activity is at the time the fly is about to hatch and the nymphs are usually a mottled brownish-red color as indicated in the fly above. The fly is best as fished in the sub-surface film of the pond or lake when cruising fish are looking for easy prey. Many streams in the west such as the Firehold have heavy vegetation which contains a good population of damsel flies.

DRESSING

HOOK—Mustad #9672
SIZE—6-8-10
THREAD—Pre-waxed brown nylon
TAILS—Three red-brown hackle points
BODY—Fur dubbed reddish brown fox and Australian possum
RIBBING—Brown thread
LEGS—English grouse
COVERT—Small piece of English grouse

GIANT BLACK STONEFLY

HISTORY AND ORIGIN

Most serious anglers know you have to get down deep with a nymph to be successful and often this will cause the loss of flies. Many anglers do not use flies that are big enough, thus they very often only land small to medium-sized fish. A good start for any angler East or West. On this pattern we have chosen to use angora wool for the body for it is not as easy to dub fur bodies on such large hooks. The basic shape and outline is suggestive of many types of food forms that are available to trout and salmon. Our shop first sold these flies in 1974 and come in various color schemes. We have used this style of fly for many years and it's amazing to see a small trout devour such a large fly. It's even more exciting to feel a big one on the other end of the leader. Don't be discouraged, keep the fly deep on the bottom.

DRESSING

HOOK—Mustad #38941 or #9672
SIZE—2-4-6-8
THREAD—Black monocord
TAIL—Black ostrich herl
BODY—Black angora wool
LEGS—Black hackle
COVERT—Black goose
THORAX—Black angora wool

BACKSWIMMER

HISTORY AND ORIGIN

In "Fishing Flies and Fly Tying," Bill Blades gives an excellent pattern for the Backswimmer. This book is a must for tyers who want to make flies that are exact copies of the natural. During the latter part of the season this can be a very important fly, especially for pond fishing. Be careful in trying to gather the naturals for they give a nasty bite. If you look carefully at the water on ponds late in the season you will see many small insects seeming to swim upside-down with small oar-like legs. These are backswimmers and waterboatmen. Often when fish are rising on ponds in this late season they are taking this fly and will refuse any fly but a carefully-tied backswimmer and waterboatman. They have a basic beetle shape and come in assorted colors and sizes.

DRESSING

HOOK—Mustad #94840
SIZE—12-14-16
THREAD—Black pre-waxed nylon
TAIL—Moosemane, tied short and stubby
BODY—Orange seal fur dubbing saturated with cement and made black at the thorax and on the underside with black enamel
LEGS—Tan-brown hackle trimmed to shape
WINGS—Woodcock, stiffened with vinyl or clear cement

COPPER BUG

HISTORY AND ORIGIN

This original pattern by the author was entered as the author's choice of flies in open category in the 1975 International Fly Tyer's Competition sponsored by the United Fly Tyers of Boston, Mass. The choice of materials was made with the intention that most flies should be simple in basic construction and made with available materials. By using the copper wire as an intregal part of the fly we gain the copper color, which is most effective and we also gain a segment effect with the spiral wrapping of the wire on the outside of the abdomen.

DRESSING

HOOK—Mustad #38941 or #9672
SIZE—4-6-8-10-12-14-16
THREAD—Brown monocord or brown pre-waxed nylon
TAIL—Cock pheasant barbules
BODY—Wrap abdomen with one layer of #30 copper
    wire (the type used for rewiring electrical motors),
    wrap thorax with two layers of same. Then wrap
    whole body with orange floss or silk, shape to basic
    nymph shape to size of hook. Wrap abdomen with
    single wrapping of copper wire.
RIBBING—Peacock herl with fine overlay of fine gold
    oval tinsel. This will give added strength to the
    peacock herl
LEGS—Brown hackle, trimmed top and bottom
COVERT—Cock pheasant
THORAX—Peacock herl, tied full

BROWN LATEX STONEFLY

HISTORY AND ORIGIN

For the past two years the staff of Dick Surette Fly Fishing Shop, Dick Stewart, Red Peckham, and Dick Surette, have tied stoneflies with stripped goose quills, monofilament, furs, silks, and rubber materials, looking for the perfect material. We have concluded that latex is the most dyeable, usable material with unlimited potential. Any combination of light underbody and dark tops can be used to match the predominant nymphs in your area. Use dark monocord to bind the latex down and give the fly the segmented effect. Dye some deer body hair to complement your nymph's basic color tone for legs.
Hint: As the fly is completed, put one coat of pliobond cement to really set the color of the dark latex top and give the fly a "wet" appearance.

DRESSING

HOOK—Mustad #79580 (turn down slightly, forward 1/3 of hook)
SIZE—2-4-6-8-10
THREAD—Pre-waxed monocord
WEIGHT—Lead strips laid parallel to hook, then wrapped and flattened with pliers
TAILS—Brown stripped goose quills, short sides
UNDERBODY—Sparkle yarn, mohlon, or wool (sparkle yarn best)
COVERT—Strips of cut latex dyed with Pantone Marker #499
RIBBING—Dark brown monocord
LEGS—Deer body hair dyed brown

ANDROSCOGGIN GREEN CADDIS

HISTORY AND ORIGIN

The Androscoggin River near Errol, New Hampshire has a very heavy, well-regulated flow of water that is controlled by the Brown Paper Company via a series of dams at Berlin twenty miles downriver. This is one of the few rivers in New England that does not suffer the ravages of spring runoff and shifting bottoms. As a result, the insect life on the bottom is enormous in quantity and variety. During one seining session last summer we gathered the following nymphs: mayfly, stonefly, three types of dragonflies, hellgrammites, scuds, beetles, and prolific quantities of caddis larvae in olive green. In fact, we gathered over 600 specimens in slightly over one hour and missed numerous flies because of the volume of water flow.

A very important color was olive green in both caddis and dragonfly nymphs. This river is big, brawly, and difficult to wade, and a long cast against frequent winds is the order of the day. A fast full sinking line with the "Andy Caddis" can be productive, a sink tip will perform well on the emerger caddis pupa patterns.

DRESSING

HOOK—Mustad #37160 Caddis Hook
SIZES—12-14-16-18-20
THREAD—Olive pre-waxed nylon
BODY—A mixture of three-fourths Australian Possum and one-fourth #119 Olive Jorgensen Caddis Blends
HEAD—Black ostrich herl, full

BLACK DRAGONFLY

HISTORY AND ORIGIN

Today so much is written about caddis flies, mayflies, and stoneflies that we tend to overlook some very important food forms that are just as prevalent. The dragonfly is a large, tasty morsel which is readily available in most trout waters; the trout recognizes this fact but often the angler does not. The silhouette of the dragonfly is very distinctive, and by following the directions below you should be able to tie any shaped body you will ever need.

Lay lead wire along the shank of the hook, wrap another layer of wire around the parallel lead, and flatten with a small pair of pliers to form a flat weighted base. Every household has the soft plastic lids to butter or ice cream containers; save them for they make ideal material for flat nymph bodies that can be cut and shaped to any form easily. These lids are rigid enough to hold their shape, easy to work with your fly tying scissors, and, best of all, available and free.

DRESSING

HOOK—Mustad #9671
SIZES—6-8-10
THREAD—Pre-waxed black monocord
TAILS—Black ostrich, short
BODY—WEIGHTING—Lead wire parallel to shank, then flattened
      SHAPING—Cut plastic ice cream lids to desired shape
      MATERIAL—Black Angora spun fur
COVERT—Black goose quill
LEGS—Black hackle, trimmed top and bottom
THORAX—Black Angora spun fur

ADAMS

HISTORY AND ORIGIN

Leonard Halladay, of Mayfield, Michigan first tied this fly in 1922 and named it in honor of a good friend, Mr. C. F. Adams, an ardent angler on the Boardman River in Michigan. A combination of two very basic colors, brown and grizzly hackles gives a very good pattern. Many anglers have stated that if they had to use just one dry fly it would be the Adams, a better choice could not be made for this fly can represent many basic mayflies. A spent wing version is an excellent fly to be used during a spinner fall which can produce some mighty fine angling.

DRESSING

HOOK—Mustad #94840, #94833 or Orvis Supreme
SIZES—12-14-16-18-20
THREAD—Black-silk, monocord or nylon
TAIL—Evenly mixed grizzly and brown barbules
BODY—Dubbed gray muskrat body fur
WINGS—Grizzly hackle points
HACKLES—One grizzly and one brown

QUILL GORDON

HISTORY AND ORIGIN

The father of American dry fly fishing, Theodore Gordon, spent 35 years on the streams of the Catskills in upstate N.Y. working on flies and fishing tactics and one result of his efforts was the Quill Gordon. Gordon wrote numerous letters to Halford, his English counterpart, to compare notes and basic new concepts. The Quill Gordon was first used in the early 1890's and was one of the early flies in the trend towards light tackle and good imitations of American insect life. Today almost 100 years later it is still a very basic fly.

DRESSING

HOOK—Mustad #94840, #94833, or Orvis Supreme
SIZES—12-14-16-18-20
THREAD—Black-silk, monocord or nylon
TAIL—Sparse blue dun barbules
WINGS—Wood duck flanks
BODY—Stripped quill from peacock eye
RIBBING—Very fine gold wire
HACKLES—Two medium shade of blue dun

BLACK GNAT

HISTORY AND ORIGIN

A black fly is one of the oldest and best of all colors, especially in smaller sizes. This pattern and type of fly is one of the oldest in existence, dating back several hundred years. Many food particles in the stomachs of trout are distinctly on the blackish side in color. Food types such as beetles, ants, midges are just a few of the black forms of insects. A black fly was on Dame Juliana Berner's list of flies in 1486, countless black flies have been tied since that time; more will come.

DRESSING

HOOK—Mustad #94840, #94833 or Orvis Supreme
SIZES—10-12-14-16-18-20-22-24
THREAD—Pre-waxed nylon, black
TAIL—Black hackle barbules
BODY—Dyed black beaver dubbing
WING—Natural gray duck pointers
HACKLE—Two black hackles

HENDRICKSON

HISTORY AND ORIGIN

One of the truly American dry flies, tied by Roy Steenrod of Liberty, N.Y. and named for one of his good customers, A. E. Hendrickson. This pattern emerged in 1915 and is a most popular pattern and a great fly on the first hatches of spring when the fish are not as wary as they will be later on in the season. The Hendrickson is a steady emerger and comes in great numbers, it is one of the few mayflies that will arouse the big fish to the surface during the daytime hatches of spring. This is usually April and May for Pa. and N.Y. and May and June for Maine, N.H. and Vt.

DRESSING

HOOK—Mustad #94840, #94833, Orvis Supreme
SIZES—12-14-16-18-20
THREAD—Black-silk, monocord or nylon
TAIL—Blue dun barbules
BODY—Pink creamy fur from the belly area of a vixen fox, area that has urine stain
WINGS—Wood duck
HACKLE—Watery blue dun

LIGHT CAHILL

HISTORY AND ORIGIN

A fishing railroad man, Dan Cahill of Port Jervis, N.Y. first originated this fly. Later the light-colored fly was tied by Theodore Gordon and then adapted to today's pattern by William Chandler on the Neversink in upstate N. Y. Dan Cahill first evolved the pattern in the 1880's. The present day pattern is very light in coloration as compared to earlier versions, the Light Cahill is a favorite fly of many anglers and the hatch of Light Cahills is a major hatch on many streams in the U. S. Effective in many sizes and a most visible fly.

DRESSING

HOOK—Mustad #94840, #94833 or Orvis Supreme
SIZES—10-12-14-16-18-20
THREAD—Cream or yellow
TAIL—Light ginger barbules
BODY—Light creamy red fox belly
WINGS—Wood duck flank
HACKLE—Very light ginger

GRASSHOPPER

HISTORY AND ORIGIN

All fly tyers have a version of the grasshopper and new patterns appear every year. First noted in angling literature in 1653 by the "Compleat Angler" by Walton as one of the twelve flies that all anglers should have in their kits. Hundreds of flies of this type have been tied in the past few hundred years and I feel it is taken mostly by trout and salmon as a superb copy of the caddis fly with its basic tent shape and down wing. The pattern given below is the most popular of the many patterns available.

DRESSING

HOOKS—Mustad #9671, #9672, #94840, #3906B
SIZES—4-6-8-10-12-14-16
THREAD—Black-silk or pre-waxed nylon
TAIL—Red hackle barbules
TAIL LOOP—Small loop of body material
BODY—Orange, yellow or green
RIBBING—Badger hackle
WING—Mottled turkey, downwing, lacquered
HACKLE—Coachman brown, slightly collared

FAN WING ROYAL COACHMAN

HISTORY AND ORIGIN

As an attractor and locator of trout, the fan wing is tops, also a classic fly of great beauty, tied as a variation of the standard Royal Coachman, many have great faith in the Fan Wing Royal. F. M. Halford is first credited with the fan wing for dry flies by the 1889 edition of "Dry Fly Fishing." A fan wing is not easy to cast, it tends to spin and can cause knots in your leader, but this is only a minor problem. Probably the best known dry fly on a world wide basis and used wherever trout are found.

DRESSING

HOOK—Mustad #94840
SIZES—6-8-10-12-14
THREAD—Black-silk
TAIL—Golden pheasant tippets
BODY—Peacock herl, red silk, peacock herl
WINGS—Two white breast feathers from male wood duck
HACKLE—Two coachman brown hackles

GRIZZLY RIFFLE FLY

HISTORY AND ORIGIN

A fly designed by the author for fishing on the Saco River for big browns during the evening rise. A combination of basic mayfly colors, form and style make this series of flies our personal favorites. The wings, hackle, and tail are tied slightly oversize to enable the angler to see the fly readily in the failing light of dusk. Thus the angler can place the fly right on the trout's nose, a most important factor in brown trout fishing especially for wise big old brownies. First tied in 1964, these flies float extremely well, all tied with fur bodies and a little longer hook that will support heavy hackling. Most effective on riffle runs and broken water where trout will feed just prior to sunset as they move into their feeding stations. This is a durable, good floater that can be seen well after sunset and you can follow the fly as it approaches the fish. Try this pattern and you will catch fish. See note below.

DRESSING

HOOK—Mustad #9671
SIZE—10-12-14-16
THREAD—Pre-waxed black nylon
TAIL—White impali, full
BODY—Natural muskrat, full
WING—White impali, tied one size larger than hook size
HACKLE—Three grizzly hackles, tied full
NOTE—This fly also comes in gray, ginger, brown, black, cream.

HUMPY

HISTORY AND ORIGIN

This dry fly is probably the best known dry fly pattern in the west. Credit is given to Jack Horner of California for the style of tying and many variations have come along. The name Humpy was originated in the Jackson Hole area of Wyoming. The Humpy is designed to float in big rough waters where the usual dry fly would be pulled under after a few feet of drift. The Humpy will enable the angler to reach spots that are impossible to reach with the standard flies. The body is made by wrapping over the wing material many times. Body color should take on the color of the head color. This is a fly that can be most effective on any large river in the East as well as the West.

DRESSING

HOOK—Mustad #94840
SIZE—4-6-8-10-12-14-16
THREAD—Monocord, all thread to match body color
TAIL—Dark elk hair
BODY—Upper body—deer hair or elk hair Under
    Body—Monocord—black, yellow, red, orange,
    fluorescent green or fluorescent orange.
WING—Tips of hair used for the body are also used as the
    wings for this fly
HACKLE—Badger preferred, can be grizzly and brown
    mixed, ginger, blue dun or black.

MOSQUITO

HISTORY AND ORIGIN

Here we have a good dry fly pattern that will take trout but the adult insect is really not on the surface in any quantity to really provide any angling. This fly is just a good looking imitation that could fall into many different types of flies that fall on the water. It may even resemble a caddis adult more than a mayfly. This is a pattern that came to the colonies with the English many years ago and is just as effective today. The broken light pattern that is given off by the salt and pepper effect of the grizzly materials are most assuredly one of the best choices of materials for any fly. This is one reason why grizzly is in such demand as a basic fly tying material. This fly in a wide range of sizes is a good basic dry fly to have in your boxes.

DRESSING

HOOK—Mustad #94840
SIZE—8-10-12-14-16-18-20
THREAD—Black pre-waxed nylon
TAIL—Grizzly barbules
BODY—One white and one dark moose mane, wound at same time for segments
HACKLE—Two grizzly hackles
WINGS—Two grizzly points

GRAY CADDIS

HISTORY AND ORIGIN

For several years I have felt that the dry imitations of the caddis were not durable enough to be skittered and danced across the riffles as the naturals will. With this Gray Caddis we have a good floating caddis that is also a down wing to give the appearance of a caddis natural. We have used some of the principles in the Humpy style of tying and the down wings and added a hackle for further floatability, the result is the Gray Caddis as pictured above. The small pieces of elk and deer hair will really float but the overall fly is still as delicate as the caddis naturals appear. This fly is also effective as it first goes under at the end of a long drift. Sometimes trout will think that the fly is trying to emerge from the surface film and has just submerged. Bounce this pattern along the riffles and fast water and you certainly will take fish. Can be also tied any color scheme to best imitate the naturals in your area.

DRESSING

HOOK—Mustad #94840
SIZE—10-12-14-16
THREAD—Gray pre-waxed nylon
TAIL—Blue dun barbules
BODY—Underbody—muskrat or Orvis #26 brown olive
      spectrablend—Overbody—gray tone deer body hair
WING—Blue dun barbules, down wing style
HACKLE—Blue dun

GRAY FOX

HISTORY AND ORIGIN

All serious fly tyers should have a copy of "A Book of Trout Flies" by Preston Jennings. This was the first serious book on fly tying and gives valuable information on hatches, dates, and little known facts about trout insects. The dressings on flies are clear, concise and easy to work with. In the 1920's Mr. Jennings worked out this pattern and for the lack of any formal name he called it the Gray Fox. It is actually the *Stenonema fuscum* which hatches along with the *Stenonema vicarium* or March Brown but is smaller. This fly like the March Brown has wings that slant backward in an unusual manner. Both the Gray Fox and March Brown hatch in late May and June in New England.

DRESSING

HOOK—Mustad #94840
SIZE—10-12-14-16-18
THREAD—Primrose
TAIL—Ginger game cock barbules
BODY—Light red fox fur from red fox belly
WINGS—Flank feather from mallard drake
HACKLE—Ginger with light grizzly

CREAM SACO CADDIS

HISTORY AND ORIGIN

This is an original pattern from our shop. In early spring one of the first flies to appear is a small cream-colored caddis fly. This fly will hover over the riffles and fast water in early spring and make a fleeting appearance on the surface of the water. Let the fly float for a short distance before you pick up the fly for another cast. It does not hurt your chance to make this fly skitter along in an erratic fashion. The overall appearance of this fly is the adult caddis fly that has hatched and is flitting on the surface of the streams. It is most effective fished upstream on a dead drift with a slight twitch now and then. As it swings around you can pop it under at the end of the drift. A fish will often follow the fly for a distance and take the fly just as it pops under at the end of the float.

DRESSING

HOOK—Mustad #94840
SIZE—10-12-14-16
THREAD—Primrose yellow pre-waxed nylon
TAIL—Creamy elk barbules
BODY—Overbody—creamy colored elk body, tied
    Humpy style—Underbody—#3 Orvis sulphur Spec-
    trablend
WING—Ginger barbules, tied downwing style
HACKLE—Ginger

HENRYVILLE

HISTORY AND ORIGIN

A very popular caddis dry fly imitation first tied by Hiram Brobst of Leighton, Pa. for use on the private waters of the Henryville Club. "American Trout Fishing" by the Theodore Gordon Club of New York contains a very good chapter on the Henryville Club waters and the dressing of the fly by Ernest Schweibert. The Henryville Club waters were on the Brodheads Creek of the Poconos of Pennsylvania and formed an important saga in the development of this fly as well as several other patterns. First introduced to our staff of fly tyers by our head resident fly tyer, Dick Stewart, who is a native of Pennsylvania. At present it is our most effective dry caddis pattern and equally good as a wet fly just under the surface. The original pattern had either red floss or chocolate brown body. Small modifications such as making a dubbed olive fur body have improved the fly many times over to hundreds of anglers.

DRESSING

HOOK—Mustad #94840
SIZES—12-14-16-18-20
THREAD—Tan pre-waxed nylon
BODY—Olive dubbed fur
RIBBING—Grizzly hackle, palmered
UNDERWING—5-6 strands of wood duck flank ending
    beyond bend of hook
OVERWING—Two sections of slate gray mallard quill,
    tied downwing tent style.
HACKLE—Dark ginger

HAIRWING CADDIS

HISTORY AND ORIGIN

The hairwing caddis has come into its own during the 1970's with the publication of a few books among the best of which is "The Caddis and the Angler" by Eric Leiser and Larry Solomon, with its research on caddis life cycles and habits. By utilizing relatively available materials and solid, less complicated fly tying procedures, caddis fly patterns can easily be formed. With more pollution, higher water temperatures, and less trout water with fewer mayflies, the caddis becomes increasingly important.

Materials such as mink tails are now available in a wide range of colors; with Rit dye any color can be made quickly to suit the angler's needs.

Caddis larval and pupal imitations that are used at the proper depths by probing with a sink tip, nymph tip, or any of the wide variety of sinking lines will reap benefits for the serious angler. Put the fly in the proper place at the right time and the caddis fly is a killer fly pattern.

DRESSING

HOOK—Mustad #94840
SIZES—12-14-16-18-20
THREAD—Pre-waxed nylon, to match the basic overall
    color of the fly
BODY—Dubbed fur, to match basic color of fly
WING—Dyed mink, tied downwing. Take a white mink tail
    and dye to your specifications.
HACKLE—To match the basic color of your fly

SACO RED QUILL

HISTORY AND ORIGIN

In the upper parts of northern New England and Canada the fly hatches can be quite a bit later than stated in most previous literature. Often you can add three to five weeks to some of the emergence charts that were basically designed for the Catskills, Adirondacks, and parts of Pennsylvania. Some of our higher mountain ponds do not clear of ice till May after a severe winter, the same is true of a few of our lakes. Adjust your schedule to fit local needs.

Hendrickson time is usually the first week in June to the end of June; this is the hatch on the Saco River system in the White Mountains of New Hampshire. By this time the rivers have dropped to the proper levels and the water has warmed to over 50 degrees, the magic temperature for fly hatches.

DRESSING

HOOK—Mustad #94840
SIZES—12-14-16-18
THREAD—Pre-waxed black nylon
TAIL—Rusty dun hackle barbules
BODY—Reddish/brown peacock eye quill
RIBBING—Very fine gold wire
WINGS—Blue dun hackle points
HACKLE—Rusty dun

BLUE WING OLIVE DUN

HISTORY AND ORIGIN

As early summer moves forward the hatches begin to dwindle from the May/June frenzy of feeding. This is the time for mayflies such as the Blue Wing Olive—a smaller hatch but nonetheless steady and important to the observant angler—to come into their own.

The Blue Wing Olive is on the small side, size 14 to 18, and it can take serious looking and study to locate and identify this diminutive mayfly. The natural insect will hatch sparsely all day long and will pick up intensity at dusk. In addition spinners from the previous few days' activity will cause a significant flurry of rising trout at twilight to dark. This is a late season fly emerging during late June and well into the whole month of July.

Quite often when we see trout on the prowl and rising, we assume they are taking duns right on the surface. With careful study you will notice that they are taking the nymphal form just under the surface and the nymph pattern is the fly to use.

DRESSING

HOOK—Mustad #94940 or #94833
SIZES—14-16-18-20
THREAD—Olive pre-waxed nylon
TAIL—Medium blue dun hackle barbules
WINGS—Dark bluish dun hackle points
BODY—Pale olive/yellowish wool and red fox mixed
    dubbing
HACKLE—Medium blue dun

MUDDLER

HISTORY AND ORIGIN

Professional fly tyer, Don Gapen of Anoka, Minn., originated this pattern for the Nipigon River in Ontario to copy a fresh water sculpin. This has been the most popular American pattern in the past 30 years, good all over North America and now being used in other parts of the world. Drab and sombre but a killing pattern for trout and salmon, it is most used on the bottom, but can be successfully used on the top. This fly could imitate many kinds of food that abound in the lower reaches of trout environment.

DRESSING

HOOK—Mustad #9672, #9671, #38941
SIZES—1/0-2-4-6-8-10-12-14
THREAD—Black, heavier than usual for hook size
TAIL—Pair of mottled turkey quills
BODY—Gold tinsel, double-wrapped, short
Wing—Gray squirrel tail or brown impali, over which is tied a pair of mottled turkey wings, upright
HEAD— Deer body, natural grayish tan, small bunches tied securely in and all around the hook. You need 5 or 6 bunches, tied in and clipped to desired shape. Leave some long.

HORNBERG

HISTORY AND ORIGIN

The Hornberg was first tied as a caddis fly imitation by Frank Hornberg of Michigan in the early 1950's to match the caddis hatches in that area. A basic tent shape fly that is now tied in a variety of colors that can be tied wet or dry and is equally effective. Most frequently used along the bottom of the area being fished. Original wing was mallard but is now tied yellow, cinnamon, blue, natural woodduck, bronze mallard and green. The most popular fly in northern New England for the past twenty years, now used over much of U.S.

DRESSING

HOOK—Mustad #9671 or #94840
SIZES—2-4-6-8-10-12-14
BODY—Silver tinsel flat
UNDERWING—Yellow impali or yellow hackle barbules, faintly showing
OUTERWING—Two mallard flanks, tied flat and tent shape over the underwing, sometimes lacquered to gain tent shape
CHEEKS—Jungle cock or substitute
HACKLES—Two soft grizzly, dry fly style, tied collar style or flared back
THREAD—Black-silk

WHITLOCK SCULPIN

HISTORY AND ORIGIN

An updated version of the Muddler, by Dave Whitlock of Oklahoma has come on the fly tyer scene in the early 1970's. This fly is a more exact copy of the sculpin and a bit more difficult to tie. Care must be taken with this fly so the pattern will react as it is designated. You may have to tie this pattern several times before you feel that you have mastered the fly. This fly is very adequately described in "The Master Fly Tying Guide" by Art Flick, other variations and versions will come along to make the fly better.

DRESSING

HOOK—Mustad #9672 or #38941
SIZES—1/0-2-4-6-8
THREAD—Light orange
BODY WEIGHT—Lead wire
BODY—A rich yellowish cream, light amber seal, yellow
    seal, tan fox, white rabbit
WING—Two dyed brown grizzly saddles, tied flat
RIBBING—Gold oval rib.
UNDERWING—Red fox squirrel tail
GILLS—Red wool dubbing
PECTORAL FINS—Fans of hen mallard
COLLAR—Deer body hair, natural light dun brown,
    tinted yellow, golden brown and dark brown deer
    body.
HEAD—Same as collar

HISTORY AND ORIGIN

This fly is a favorite of Larry Roy a former tackle store operator in Salem, N.H. The fly originated in the Sebago Lake area in 1971 by some of the local guides for trout and salmon. On a trip to Pittsburg, N.H. the fly was used on Perry Stream and Indian Stream with great success. One fly took 88 trout in two days of fishing, hence the name "88". Being a down wing this takes the appearance of a caddis fly and is very effective wet or dry. The pictured version is weighted with fine red brass wire, the unweighted fly is tied with fluorescent orange wool. This fly is particularly good for brookies in pond fishing but is equally effective on streams and rivers. Give this a try.

DRESSING

HOOK—Mustad #9671
SIZE—10-12-14
THREAD—Pre-waxed brown nylon
BODY—Rear two thirds, fine red brass wire—Front third-green floss
WINGS—Lemon side wood duck
HACKLE—One grizzly on wet style, two on dry fly

DARK HORNBURG

HISTORY AND ORIGIN

Back Lake is a fairly shallow body of water (maximum sounded depth is 14 feet), but it is laden with vegetation that provides oxygen and shelter for aquatic life. A good-sized dark caddis is very abundant and will emerge in great numbers to provide quality dry fly angling to cruising rainbows. This fly is approximately hook size #6, 2x long, a downwing pattern that is styled along the Hornburg proportions.

Of all flies in existence the Hornburg is probably the easiest to use; you cannot fish this fly improperly. The pattern works on the surface as a dry caddis, slightly under as an emerger; on the bottom with a sinking line it is deadly in a variety of retrieves.

The Dark Hornburg was devised in 1975 by the author on one of his "upcountry" trips to Pittsburg to imitate the hatching dark caddis of Back Lake. Fly tyers can use this basic style to imitate any caddis pattern found in their particular area. Experiment; you won't be sorry.

DRESSING

HOOK—Mustad #9671 2x long
SIZES—4-6-7-10-12-14
THREAD—Brown pre-waxed nylon
BODY—Creamy tan polypropylene or Australian possum
WING—Bottom layer—mallard dyed wood duck
          Top layer—bronze mallard or chocolate dyed brown mallard
HACKLE—One coachman brown and one dark blue dun

BLACK ANT

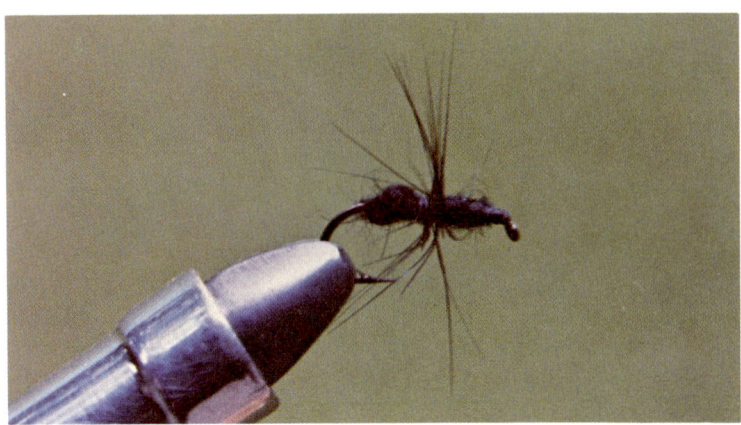

HISTORY AND ORIGIN

Marryatt and Halford in the 1800's and Hewitt in the early 1900's and the tyers in Pennsylvania in the late 1940's and early 1950's all worked on ant patterns. Ants can be a very important food fare, especially as the season dwindles and the mayfly and caddis fly hatches wane. This fly is another pattern that is constantly being worked upon and as new materials are developed usually new patterns emerge. Ants should be a very basic fly in all anglers boxes.

DRESSING

HOOKS—Mustad #94840, #94842, #94833
SIZES—12-14-16-18-20-22
THREAD—Black-silk or pre-waxed nylon
ABDOMEN—Black beaver, dubbed
LEGS—Black hackle, sparse, tied in middle
THORAX—Black beaver, dubbed, tied full

JASSID

HISTORY AND ORIGIN

In "A Modern Dry Fly Code" by Vince Marinaro describes the Jassid, named after the class of insects Jassidae, now changed to Cicadellidae. Marinaro chose the former to name the Jassid. Tied to copy small forms of food just under the surface film, as fish will rise and take this form of food awash, and not on the surface as suspected. A very good fly for late season angling when the trout are selective.

DRESSING

HOOK—Mustad #94840, #94842, #94833
SIZES—16-18-20-22-24
BODY—Tying silk, any color
THREAD—To match body color
HACKLE—One ginger, wound as ribbing along entire
    length of body
WING—Single jungle cock eye

BLUE CHARM

HISTORY AND ORIGIN

A very basic fly in any serious salmon angler's selection. This fly was brought from England many years ago and is one of the best Atlantic Salmon patterns. The angler who developed the greased line method of Salmon fly fishing was Mr. A.H. Wood, an Englishman who felt the manner of presentation and line of drift was more important than the fly pattern. For one whole year he used a Blue Charm and by varying the sizes only, his average for landed salmon stayed about the same as in prior years, and in fact it improved on certain days of the season.

DRESSING

HOOK—Mustad #36890, #36814 or #3582C
SIZES—4-6-8-10-12
THREAD—Black-silk
TAG—Fine silver tinsel
TAIL—Golden pheasant crest, curving upward
BUTT—Black ostrich herl
BODY—Black-silk floss
RIBBING—Oval silver tinsel
THROAT—Collar style, silver doctor blue
WING—Bronze mallard, over which are sparse strips of
    teal flanks
TOPPING—Golden pheasant crest

COSSEBOOM

HISTORY AND ORIGIN

One of the simple hairwing flies as originated by an insurance executive from Rhode Island, Mr. John Cosseboom in the early 1920's. Using simple basic procedures and gray squirrel wing, this American hairwing was an early pattern in the trend towards simplification of salmon flies, and away from fancy English patterns. Gray squirrel, fitch, impala, bear and similar materials are the backbone of the American style hairwings, single or double hook. This has become a staple fly in very many Atlantic Salmon anglers fly boxes.

DRESSING

HOOK—Mustad #36890, #3582C
SIZES—3/0-2/0-1/0-2-4-6-8-10-12
TAG—Silver tinsel, embossed
TAIL—Olive green silk floss, short
BODY—Olive green silk floss
RIB—Silver tinsel, embossed
WING—Gray squirrel, long as tail
HACKLE—Collar style, lemon yellow hackle
THREAD—Pre-waxed red nylon, lacquered

BUTTERFLY

HISTORY AND ORIGIN

For the past several years this has been the most used and most successful fly on the Miramichi system of New Brunswick. Originated by Maurice Ingalls of Florida, it is also called the Ingalls Butterfly. Styled after the Coachman fly, this is another simple hairwing, but the hair in this fly calls for hair from a young goat; this seems to pulsate and have more breathing in the wings. Tied in small sizes this is a very good low water pattern, an offset bronzed hook is usually used, various colored butts can be added as a variation.

DRESSING

HOOK—Mustad #7958, #3906
SIZES—4-6-8-10-12
THREAD—Black-silk
TAIL—Red hackle barbules, fairly long
BODY—Peacock herl, rusty color
WINGS—Goat, splayed at 30 degrees, slanted back, dressed sparsely
HACKLES—Tied sparse, brown coachman, one turn behind wings, one turn in front

BLACK BEAR-GREEN BUTT

HISTORY AND ORIGIN

Harry Smith of Cherryfield, Maine was the originator of the Black Bear series of hairwing flies in the 1920's. Black is always a good color for Atlantic salmon and the added spice of a colored butt is also attractive to the salmon. The butts can be orange, red, yellow or green and the fluorescent colors are effective. Fitch-dyed squirrel, black monkey and skunk can also be used for the black hairwing. This style of salmon fly is basically American and is the easiest to tie in terms of salmon patterns. They are good flies all over the world.

DRESSING

HOOK—Mustad #36890, #3582C or #3906
SIZES—4-6-8-10
THREAD—Black-silk
TAG—Flat silver tinsel
TAIL—Black hackle barbules
BUTT—Green Fluorescent wool or nylon
BODY—Black-silk floss or black seal
RIBBING—Oval silver tinsel
WING—Black bear, sparse
HACKLE—Black, collar style

RUSTY RAT

HISTORY AND ORIGIN

In the early 1900's, Mr. Roy A. Thompson originated the series of rat flies. By taking the first initial of each name, we have the abbreviations "rat," short for Roy A. Thompson. This is one of the earliest of the hairwing patterns for Atlantic Salmon. There were nine basic patterns in the original series and many variations have been worked out. The Rusty Rat was originated by Dr. Orrin Summers of New Jersey, and is a very good fly to be used in high discolored water where a visible fly is essential to catching fish. Today, the rat series is widely used.

DRESSING

HOOK—Mustad #36890, #3582C
SIZES—2-4-6-8-10
THREAD—Pre-waxed red nylon, lacquered
TAG—Gold oval tinsel
TAIL—Peacock sword, tied short
BODY—Rear half, bright yellow floss, front half, peacock herl, a length of yellow floss should extend to end of body as a veiling to end of body (see color plate)
WING—Sparse gray fox guard hairs
HACKLE—Grizzly, collar style

BLACK FITCHTAIL

HISTORY AND ORIGIN

Ernest Schwiebert, one of America's most articulate and knowledgeable anglers has described the Fitchtail in the excellent book, "Master Fly Tying Guide," edited by Art Flick. By taking the basic color of the Black Fairy and Orange Butt, he has put a softer wing material, the fitchtail, which comes in many shades and hues. This fly has been readily accepted by the angling public and the fitchtails have been difficult to obtain. A very simple pattern to tie, more will be coming along in the next few years, of course it is a good salmon fly.

DRESSING

HOOKS—Mustad #36890, #3582C
SIZES—3/0-2/0-1/0-2-4-6-8-10
THREAD—Black-silk
TIP—Bright orange yellow floss
TAG—Silver tinsel
TAIL—Golden pheasant crest
BODY—Black rayon floss
RIBBING—Flat silver tinsel
THROAT—Black hackle fibers
WING—Black fitchtail

PASS LAKE

HISTORY AND ORIGIN

This pattern was supplied by Bruce Raymer of Goose Bay Outfitters who is fortunate enough to be able to fish for giant brookies and Atlantic salmon everyday in the Labrador wilderness. The fishing is every bit as good as you have read about. This is a local pattern used by the natives in the Eagle River section of Labrador which is located 150 air miles south east of Goose Bay. As you can see from the photo the fly is very simple and basic which has become very predominant in today's dressing of salmon flies. This fly seems to become more effective as it is used and torn apart. The light pattern will change on the fly with use and sometimes just a bare, faint resemblance of the actual fly remains. These are treasures of the angling world.

DRESSING

HOOK—#10 or #12 Atlantic salmon double
THREAD—Black silk
TAIL—Brown hackle fibers
BODY—Black chenille
WING—Single wing of white impala, wet fly style
THROAT—Brown hackle

BRONSON'S BARRISTER

HISTORY AND ORIGIN

A very simple basic salmon fly tied by Dick Surette in late 1974 for a group of lawyers or barristers in Montreal. The basic colors of black and white are also the colors for the legal profession. This fly was very successful up in Canadian waters this summer and is particularly effective as tied as a double. The wing is sparse and you can use either black squirrel, fitch or a very dark woodchuck tail, wing should be short as in all Atlantic salmon flies ending even with the bend of the hook. Worked best on dark cloudy days on fish that have been in the river for some time. A topping of golden pheasant crest can add a little color and life to the fly should you want to dress it up somewhat.

DRESSING

HOOK—#3582C or #36890
SIZE—2-4-6-8-10
THREAD—Black pre-waxed nylon
TAG—Three turns of oval silver tinsel
TAIL—Golden pheasant crest
BODY—Black wool
RIBBING—Oval silver tinsel
HACKLE—One black and one white hackle, tied collar
    style
WING—Black squirrel, fitch or woodchuck
OPTIONAL—Gold pheasant crest

HOOT SMITH SPECIAL

HISTORY AND ORIGIN

This Atlantic salmon hairwing pattern was originated and tied by "Hoot Smith," a registered guide and owner of the Governor's Table Camps of Hartland, New Brunswick. First tied in the mid 1960's, this pattern reflects the modern approach to simplified salmon dressings. Slim, well proportioned, and tied with readily available materials, it is a very basic style that is a steady producer on salmon waters.

Hoot stated: "Many people tie flies for looks but I always try to make a fly that catches fish. I like my flies on the skimpy, sparse side. The preferred wing material is black Russian squirrel but is very hard to obtain; dark fitch tail or dyed black squirrel can be substituted. The proper body color is most important and should be fluorescent pink; an optional version is with a black hackle collar."

The simple hairwing salmon fly is becoming the standard fly on many rivers. Several trout patterns tied hairwing style are good salmon flies—namely, Professor, Royal Coachman, Coachman, and March Brown, all tied with hairwings in place of quill wings.

DRESSING

HOOK—Mustad #36890 or Mustad #3582C doubles
SIZES—6-8-10
THREAD—Black silk or pre-waxed nylon
TAG—Medium oval silver tinsel
BODY—Fluorescent pink, Danville depth ray wool
RIBBING—Medium oval silver tinsel
WING—Black Russian squirrel, dark fitch tail, or dyed black squirrel.

ROGER'S FANCY

HISTORY AND ORIGIN

One of Canada's finest fly tyers, Shirley E. Woods, introduced the Roger's Fancy in the "Atlantic Salmon Journal" in the January 1975 issue. A greenish-toned hairwing fly with a grayish wing which is continuing the Cosseboom tradition of great flies, the above combination is very popular.

The most common fault with poorly tied Atlantic salmon flies is making the wing too long. The proper wing length is shown in this color plate; a long wing will induce short strikes. The wing should extend to the end of the hook.

DRESSING

HOOK—Mustad #36890

SIZES—2-4-6-8-10

THREAD—Black monocord

TAG—Oval silver tinsel followed by floss, both to be lacquered

TAIL—Short strands of peacock sword (not to extend beyond the wing)

BODY—Kelly green mohair or seal, ribbed with oval silver tinsel

HACKLE—Highlander green over bright yellow, both tied as beard

WING—Mixed black/white fox or combination such as silver monkey and badger. Length not to extend beyond the bend. Do not use calftail as glassy-fibered spurs are superior because of their translucence.

CHEEKS—Junglecock or a good substitute such as a slip of barred wood duck feather

HEAD—Black lacquer such as Cellaire

GRAY WULFF

HISTORY AND ORIGIN

In 1929 Lee Wulff worked out the dry flies that are named after him. One of America's veteran anglers, he has traveled far and wide in the pursuit of trout and salmon. This fly should be tied full and bulky, so to present a tasty morsel to the fish. A good floating fly especially for the fast rock strewn rivers on the salmon rivers of the far north country. This is a durable and dependable fly that has been a proven fish producer for many years. This is known as a hairwing dry fly, also good in trout sizes for trout.

DRESSING

HOOK—Wilson Atlantic Salmon Dry
SIZES—4-6-8-10
THREAD—Black-silk
TAIL—Natural brown bucktail
BODY—Blue gray muskrat dubbing
WINGS—Natural brown bucktail
HACKLE—Blue dun, four for larger sizes and three for
    smaller sizes

PINK LADY PALMER

HISTORY AND ORIGIN

A historic party of four anglers, Roy A. Thompson, Colonel Ambrose Monell, Dr. Orrin Summers, and George LaBranche worked on dry fly patterns on the Upsalquitch in New Brunswick around 1910. By 1924 the flies were proven and well tested and were presented in LaBranche's book the "Dry Fly and the Salmon." Many anglers were doubtful that the dry would work on salmon, but this party of four fished in New Brunswick when the fish were plentiful and more cooperative than today.

DRESSING

HOOK—Wilson dry fly
SIZES—4-6-8-10
THREAD—Black-silk
TAIL—Ginger colored hackle barbules
BODY—Light pink silk
RIBBING—Flat gold tinsel
HACKLE—Ginger, palmer style and light yellow at head
    of fly, 6 ginger, 1 yellow hackle

RAT FACE Mac DOUGAL

HISTORY AND ORIGIN

Harry Darbee of Livingston Manor, N.Y. tied this as a trout fly in the 1930's and it was later adapted for Atlantic Salmon. A rugged sure floater, it is a good fly for the difficult rivers of the salmon country that flow so swiftly to the ocean. The clipped deer hair body really makes this fly float for a long time in very turbulent water. One of the staple items in the dry fly boxes of many salmon fishermen. Since this fly has come along, many flies have been tied using the clipped deer hair bodies for their floating ability.

DRESSING

HOOK—Wilson Atlantic salmon dry
SIZES—4-6-8-10
THREAD—Black-silk
TAIL—Brown bucktail
BODY—Clipped brown deer body hair, egg shape
WINGS—White calf tail or grizzly points
HACKLES—Ginger or grizzly and brown mixed

MacINTOSH

HISTORY AND ORIGIN

This dry fly is of Nova Scotia origin by a group of angling brothers, the MacIntosh brothers, of Sherbrooke, Nova Scotia. These brothers were good guides who also were good anglers who tied flies in the winter; this fly was born about 1940. This fly is slightly different from the usual dry fly in structure and appearance, but it is a good floating fly that has taken many fish. Today many of the western style flies have its basic shape and characteristics. Now termed a down wing hair dry fly.

DRESSING

HOOK—Wilson dry fly or Mustad #79580
SIZES—2-4-6-8-10
TAIL—Fox squirrel, full and bushy
BODY—None
WINGS—None
HACKLE—Dark ginger or light red brown
THREAD—Black-silk

BOMBER

HISTORY AND ORIGIN

Rev. Elmer Smith in 1967 worked out this fly for the Miramichi area of New Brunswick; it is to be skittered across the surface in a dragging fashion as it finishes its cross current swing. The clipped deer hair body makes it float well. Tied on a 4x long hook, it looks odd, but it does take fish. The Buck Bug is a close relative of this pattern. A very good new salmon pattern that has come along in the past few years; most killing in larger sizes.

DRESSING

HOOK—Mustad #79580 or Wilson Dry Fly
SIZES—2-4-6
THREAD—To match body color
TAIL—Deer body, short and full
BODY—Deer body, clipped cigar shaped as in tying muddler heads, leave room so fly can hook fish properly
RIBBING—Brown hackle, palmer style, full length of body
NOTE— Place some deer body forward as in photo, to make the fly ride upright better.

SKITTERBUG

HISTORY AND ORIGIN

This pattern was originated and tied by Dick Stewart, chief resident fly tyer of the Dick Surette Fly Fishing Shop, in 1975. Each and every year we have a goodly number of requests to tie the Hewitt Skater Spider, but we always had a difficult time finding the long stiff hackles to do the job properly by our critical standards.

The ingenious method of attaching deer body hair as hackle does the job very adequately and actually makes a more durable and higher-floating fly which has definite advantages. Deer body hair is very available and is just coming into full usage as a fly tying material.

A fly such as the Skitterbug design is used as a last resort when you just can't seem to move salmon under low and warm water conditions. The salmon under these conditions is logy and prone to be at his most selective. This is the time to use the Skitterbug. Skitter and bounce the fly along the surface in a very erratic fashion; you may arouse the salmon's curiosity and a savage strike will ensue. The same fly tied in trout sizes is excellent for trout, as described in Hewitt's "Telling on the Trout."

DRESSING

HOOK—Mustad #94840 or #94833
SIZES—4-6-8-10
THREAD—Pre-waxed black monocord
BODY/HACKLE—Natural deer hair. One section spun on pointing forward tied at rear of hook. One section spun on with tips pointing to rear, tied at front of hook. Both sections pushed toward center and butts clipped.

BUC BUG

HISTORY AND ORIGIN

The trend in Atlantic salmon flies has been towards the somber colors and simple procedures. During the past few seasons a few unlikely-looking salmon flies have been most successful. First and foremost has been the Buc Bug, originated by Reverend Elmer Smith of Prince William, New Brunswick in 1970.

Reverend Smith is one of the most experienced and knowledgeable Atlantic salmon anglers in North America. His knowledge of salmon habits and fly patterns should be recorded for future generations.

The Buc Bug uses the clipped deer hair body style as in the Salmon Bomber, but the Buc Bug is a smaller low-water version. Tied originally in natural deer body hair, many other body colors and hackle ribbings are now being used and sold. The Miramichi cast will swing the fly in a swim to create a slight skittering wake and often a smashing strike or swirl. The Buc Bug is a superb new salmon fly pattern.

DRESSING

HOOK—Partridge Sproat
SIZES—6-8-10-12
THREAD—Black waxed monocord
TAIL—Fluorescent insect green
RIBBING—Brown hackle, palmered
BODY—Clipped natural deer body (Note: almost any color deer hair body would be interesting. Experiment!)

BLACK DOSE

HISTORY AND ORIGIN

This type of dressing on flies of this kind is the epitome of the art of fly tying: most difficult to tie to the proper proportions, and materials are very difficult to obtain. This pattern is a good example of the intricate salmon patterns called fancy patterns and was originated by George Kelson in the 1890's in England. This is a low water reduced dressing of the classic version.

DRESSING

HOOK—Mustad #36890, #3582C
SIZES—3/0-2/0-1/0-2-4-6-8-10
THREAD—Black-silk
TAG—Oval silver tinsel, fine
TIP—Orange silk floss, light in color
TAIL—Gold pheasant crest, over which are two married strips of teal and scarlet swan
BODY—Black silk
RIBBING—Silver tinsel, oval
HACKLE—Palmered black hackle, after tinsel
THROAT—Collar style, black hackle
WING—A pair of gold pheasant tippets, veiled with married strands of scarlet and green swan, mottled turkey
TOPPING—Golden pheasant crest
CHEEKS—Jungle cock

DURHAM RANGER

HISTORY AND ORIGIN

The Durham Ranger was originated in the early 1860's by James Wright of England and later popularized by George Kelson. A good fly to use on a dark day when salmon seem to take best. The proportion, translucency and attractiveness of this fly are its best qualities, and these traits make it hard for a salmon to resist. A clear bright day will bring out the colors ever so much better.

DRESSING

HOOK—Mustad #36890, #3582C
SIZES—3/0-2/0-1/0-2-4-6-8-10
THREAD—Black-silk
TAIL—Short silver pheasant crest, long gold pheasant crest
TAG—Silver tinsel
TIP—Yellow floss
BUTT—Black ostrich herl
BODY—Claret dubbing
RIBBING—Flat gold tinsel
HACKLE—Claret, palmered over body, blue hackle in front as throat
WINGS—Two gold pheasant tippets, long. Two tippets short, jungle cock in center of wing
CHEEKS—Light blue
TOPPING—Golden pheasant crest

DUSTY MILLER

HISTORY AND ORIGIN

Some of the salmon flies were tied to copy a theory of some of the earlier tyers that the salmon fed on butterflies and the flies had to be colorful and gaudy. We know this is not true, but still the bright and colorful patterns of the English classic style are still being used today.

DRESSING

HOOK—Mustad #36890, #3582C
SIZES—2-4-6-8-10 single or double
THREAD—Black-silk thread
TAG—Silver tinsel
TIP—Yellow silk floss
TAIL—Golden pheasant crest, Indian crow over
BUTT—Black ostrich herl
BODY—Rear two thirds, embossed silver tinsel front
  third orange silk floss
RIBBING—Silver tinsel, fine oval
THROAT—Sparse speckled gallina
WING—Pair of white tipped turkey, over which is a sheath
  of married teal, scarlet, yellow, orange swan, bustard,
  florican, and golden pheasant tail. Covered by a
  sheath of barred wood duck, narrow strips of brown
  mallard top.
TOPPING—A golden pheasant crest feather
CHEEKS—Jungle cock
HORNS—Blue and yellow macaw.

JOCK SCOTT

HISTORY AND ORIGIN

Lord John Scott's water baliff was the originator of this fly for English waters. A very good pattern that produces in low or high water, one of the oldest patterns.

DRESSING

HOOK—Mustad #36890 or #3582C
SIZES—5/0-4/0-3/0-2/0-1/0-2-4-6-8-10
THREAD—Black-silk
TAIL—Gold pheasant crest long, silver pheasant short
TAG—Silver tinsel
TIP—Yellow floss
BUTT—Black ostrich herl
BODY—Rear, yellow floss, front, black floss
RIBBING—Silver tinsel
CENTER JOINT—Black ostrich herl
TRAILERS—Gold pheasant crest, at joint
HACKLE—Guinea
WING—White tipped turkey for inner wing, outerwing is married gold pheasant tail, red, blue, and yellow strips of swan. Brown mallard, yellow and teal at top
CHEEKS—Chatterer
SHOULDERS—Jungle cock
TOPPING—Peacock sword and gold pheasant crest.

SILVER GRAY

HISTORY AND ORIGIN

Originated by James Wright of England, who won many medals and awards for his fly tying between the years of 1862 to 1883. His artistic tying won many expositions and many of his patterns are still used today over 100 years later.

DRESSING

HOOK—Mustad #36890 or #3582C
SIZES—5/0-4/0-3/0-2/0-1/0-2-4-6-8-10
THREAD—Black-silk
TAG—Silver tinsel
TIP—Two turns of silver tinsel
TAIL—A golden pheasant crest feather
BUTT—Black ostrich herl
BODY—Flat silver tinsel, over which is a badger hackle, palmer style
THROAT—Sparse teal fibers
WING—Inner wing of golden pheasant tippets, and tail fibers. Green, blue and yellow married swan. Also guinea fowl, teal. Outer wing—Bronze mallard, mallard flank
CHEEKS—Jungle cock
TOPPING—Golden pheasant crest

EASTERN DRY FLY APPENDIX

AUSABLE WULFF
HOOK—Mustad #94840
SIZES—8-10-12-14
THREAD—Red pre-waxed 6/0 nylon
TAIL—Woodchuck or moose
BODY—Bleached Australian possum
WING—White impali
HACKLE—Brown and grizzly mixed

TRICORYTHODES SPINNER
HOOK—Mustad #94840
SIZES—22-24-26
THREAD—White pre-waxed 6/0
    nylon
TAIL—White hackle barbules, 3
    only, divided
ABDOMEN—White nymph thread
THORAX—Black beaver
WINGS—White polypropelene,
    spent style

DUN VARIANT
HOOK—Mustad #94840
SIZES—10-12
THREAD—Pre-waxed gray 6/0 nylon
TAIL—Blue dun barbules
BODY—Brown hackle stem, long
    and stripped
WINGS—None
HACKLE—Dark blue dun

AMERICAN MARCH BROWN
HOOK—Mustad #94840, #94833
SIZES—10-12
THREAD—Pre-waxed orange
    6/0 nylon
TAIL—Red game cock barbules
BODY—Red fox belly mixed with
    hare's ear
WINGS—Mallard flank
HACKLE—Bright red game with
    grizzly in front

GREEN DRAKE
HOOK—Mustad #94840
SIZES—8-10-12
THREAD—Olive pre-waxed
    6/0 nylon
TAIL—Dark ginger, full and
    substantial
BODY—Creamy ginger red fox belly
RIBBING—Brown monocord
WINGS—Lemon wood duck
HACKLE—One cream, one grizzly

CREAM VARIANT
HOOK—Mustad #94833
SIZES—12-14
THREAD—Pre-waxed yellow
    6/0 nylon
TAIL—Cream hackle barbules
BODY—Cream stripped hackle stem
HACKLE—Cream, oversized
    #8 hackle

WESTERN DRY FLY APPENDIX

RENEGADE

HOOK—Mustad #94840
SIZES—4-6-8-10-12-14-16
THREAD—Black monocord
REAR HACKLE—Brown saddle
BODY—Peacock herl, tied full
FRONT HACKLE—Cream, white or
off-white saddle

RIO GRANDE KING HAIRWING

HOOK—Mustad #7957B or 3906B
SIZES—2-4-6-8 for large streams
SIZES—10-12-14-16 for small
streams
TAIL—Golden pheasant tippets
BODY—Black chenille
WING—White duck quills or calftail
HACKLE—Medium brown hackles

GRIZZLY WULFF

HOOK—Mustad #94840
SIZES—4-6-8-10-12
THREAD—Black pre-waxed
6/0 nylon
TAIL—Brown calftail
BODY—Pale yellow floss, lacquered
WING—Brown calftail
HACKLE—Mixed brown and grizzly

SOFA PILLOW

HOOK—Mustad #9671
SIZES—4-6-8-10
THREAD—Black waxed monocord
TAIL—Duck quill, red
BODY—Red wool
WING—Red squirrel
HACKLE—Dark brown, full, several
hackles

BUCKTAIL CADDIS

HOOK—Mustad #9671
SIZES—8-10-12
THREAD—Pre-waxed black nylon,
6/0
TAIL—Cock pheasant, angled
upward
BODY—Yellow wool
RIBBING—Dark ginger palmered
over body
WING—Deer body, slanted back
and up
HACKLE—Two dark ginger, full

LITTLE YELLOW STONE (female)

HOOK—Mustad #94831
SIZES—10-12-14
TAIL—Cree hackle, short
EGG SAC—Bright red, clipped short
TAIL HACKLE—Cree, one size small
BODY—Chartreuse wool or nylon,
ribbed with chartreuse A thread
HACKLE—Cree, normal size
HEAD—Chartreuse, long and flat

EASTERN WET APPENDIX

MONTREAL
HOOK—Mustad #3906
SIZES—8-10-12-14
THREAD—Black pre-waxed nylon,
    6/0
TAIL—Red duck quill
BODY—Claret floss, gold ribbing
    over
HACKLE—Claret, tied collar style
    wet
WING—Mottled turkey

BROWN HACKLE
HOOK—Mustad #3906
SIZES—8-10-12-14
TAIL—Red hackle barbules
BODY—Peacock herl, tied full
HACKLE—Brown soft-tied collar
    style
THREAD—Black pre-waxed nylon,
    6/0

GRAY HACKLE
HOOK—Mustad #3906
SIZES—8-10-12-14
THREAD—Black pre-waxed nylon
    6/0
TAIL—Red hackle barbules
BODY—Peacock herl, tied full
HACKLE—Grizzly, soft-tied collar
    style

BLUE DUN
HOOK—Mustad #3906
SIZES—8-10-12-14
THREAD—Black pre-waxed
    nylon, 6/0
TAIL—Medium blue dun barbules
BODY—Dubbed gray muskrat
    underfur
WING—Slate gray duck quill

LEISENRING SPIDER
HOOK—Mustad #3906
SIZES—12-14-16
THREAD—Hot orange pre-waxed
    nylon
TAIL—Gray partridge barbules
TAG—Hot orange pre-waxed nylon
HACKLE—Gray partridge, tied wet
    collar style

ALDER
HOOK—Mustad #3906
SIZES—8-10-12-14
THREAD—Black pre-waxed nylon,
    6/0
TAG—Flat gold mylar
BODY—Peacock herl
HACKLE—Black hen, tied wet collar
    style
WING—Mottled turkey

WESTERN WET APPENDIX

CAREY SPECIAL
HOOK—Mustad #3906B
SIZES—4-6-8-10
THREAD—Black monocord
TAIL—Several greenish/bluish ring
    neck breast feathers
BODY—Chenille—black, green
    or brown
HACKLER—Ringneck pheasant
    flank, very long

CALIFORNIA COACHMAN
HOOK—Mustad #3906
SIZES—8-10-12-14
THREAD—Pre-waxed black nylon,
    6/0
TAIL—Mallard flank fibers
BODY—Peacock herl 2/3, red
    floss 1/3
WING—White duck quill
HACKLE—Brown, tied wet style
    collar

DUCK LAKE WOOLY WORM
HOOK—Mustad #79580
SIZES—2-4-6-8
THREAD—Olive pre-waxed
    monocord
BODY—Dark olive chenille
HACKLE—Soft wet grizzly,
    palmered around total length
    of chenille body

WESTERN COACHMAN
HOOK—Mustad #7957B
SIZES—8-10-12-14
THREAD—Black monocord
TAIL—Golden pheasant tippets
BODY—Peacock herl, tied full
HACKLE—Brown soft, tied wet
    collar style

CARROT
HOOK—Mustad #7957B
SIZES—8-10-12-14
TIP—Gold flat tinsel
BODY—Orange wool, tapered
    to fullness
HACKLE—Gray or Brown partridge,
    tied wet spider style

BLONDE BURLAP
HOOK—Mustad #7070
SIZES—2-4-6-8-10
THREAD—Light tan
TAIL—Soft honey dun, short
    and full
BODY—Bleached burlap, four
    strands
HACKLE—Honey dun, wide and soft
HEAD—Tan pre-waxed nylon, long
    and tapered

EASTERN BUCKTAIL APPENDIX

TRI COLOR

HOOK—Mustad #9575
SIZES—4-6-8-10-12
THREAD—Black pre-waxed
monocord
BODY—Silver flat tinsel, oval
silver ribbing
WING—First layer—white bucktail
Second layer—orange bucktail
Third layer—green bucktail
CHEEKS—Jungle cock

DARK EDSON TIGER

HOOK—Mustad #9574 or #3665A
SIZES—4-6-8-10
THREAD—Yellow
TAG—Fine gold tinsel, narrow
TAIL—Two tips of yellow hackle
BODY—Yellow chenille, fine
THROAT—Two tips of small red
hackles
WING—Brown bucktail, dyed yellow

GRIZZLY KING HAIRWING

HOOK—Mustad #9575
SIZES—6-8-10
THREAD—Black pre-waxed
monocord
TAIL—Red goose section
BODY—Green wool or floss
WING—Gray squirrel tail
HACKLE—Grizzly, tied wet collar
style

LITTLE BROWN TROUT

HOOK—Mustad #9575
SIZES—4-6-8-10-12
THREAD—Black pre-waxed nylon,
6/0
BODY—Off-white wool, gold oval
ribbing
WING—Mixed bucktail, yellow,
orange, red and brown.
Lightest on bottom and darkest
on top

THUNDER CREEK RED FIN

HOOK—Mustad #3665A
SIZES—4-6-8-10
THREAD—Red monocord
BODY—Red floss with flat silver
ribbing
WING—Keith Fulsher/Thunder
Creek style with brown on top
and white under. Full head.
EYE—Painted yellow with black
pupil

ANDY'S SMELT

HOOK—Mustad #9575
SIZES—4-6-8-10-12
THREAD—Black pre-waxed
monocord
TAIL—Red goose section
BODY—Gold flat embossed tinsel,
gold oval ribbing
WING—Mallard flank dyed blue,
folded over tent shape for smelt
shape

WESTERN BUCKTAIL APPENDIX

PLATTE RIVER SPECIAL
HOOK—Mustad #38941
SIZES—4-6-8-10
THREAD—Brown waxed monocord
RIBBING—Embossed gold tinsel
BODY—Brown chenille
WING—Two yellow neck hackles
with a brown neck hackle at
each side. Hackles to curve
outward
HACKLE—Brown and yellow mixed,
tied back collar style wet

OLIVE MATUKA
HOOK—Mustad #79580
SIZES—4-6-8-10
RIBBING—Oval gold tinsel
BODY—Seal, spun fur tied full
WING/TAIL—Tied Matuka style from
olive soft neck hackles-2
HACKLE—Soft long olive, tied down
wet collar style
NOTE: This Matuka has been very
effective on steelhead tied
weighted and deep swimming

TROTH BULLHEAD
HOOK—Mustad #36890
SIZES—3/0-2/0-1/0-2-4-6
THREAD—Black pre-waxed monocord
TAIL—White bucktail
UPPER TAIL/BACK—Black ostrich
tied full
BODY—Dubbed cream fur
GILLS—Dubbed red fur
HEAD/HACKLE—Natural deer body
hair

SPUDDLER
HOOK—Mustad #79580
SIZES—2-4-6-8-10
THREAD—Brown pre-waxed
monocord
BODY—Cream spun wool or fur
UNDERWING—Brown calftail
UPPERWING—Grizzly dyed dark
brown
HEAD—Brown dyed antelope, spun
on and trimmed to shape

ALASKA MARY ANN
HOOK—Mustad #79580
SIZES—4-6-8-10-12
THREAD—Black pre-waxed
monocord
TAIL—Red hackle barbules
BODY—Pale tan floss, flat silver
ribbing
WING—White polar bear
CHEEKS—Jungle cock

RED TRUDE
HOOK—Mustad #79580
SIZES—2-4-6-8-10
THREAD—Black pre-waxed
monocord
BODY—Red wool, oval silver ribbing
WING—Red squirrel
HACKLE—Brown, tied collar style
wet

EASTERN STREAMER APPENDIX

RED GRAY GHOST (tandem)

HOOK—Mustad #3906, front #4 rear #6 joined by 45 pound stainless wire. Total length not to exceed 3½". Jumbos can be tied up to 6–7".

BODY—Red floss with flat silver rib

THROAT—Red bucktail over 4–6 strands of peacock herl

BEARD—Single golden pheasant crest

WING—Two medium blue dun saddles, use four for a full wing

SHOULDERS—Silver pheasant, jungle cock over

GREEN GHOST (tandem)

HOOK—Mustad #3906, front #4, rear #6

BODY—Bright orange floss, thin silver ribbing over body

THROAT—Peacock herl 4–6 strands over which are tied sparse white bucktail

WING—Green saddle hackles, four

SHOULDER—Silver pheasant

CHEEKS—Jungle cock

JOE'S SMELT

HOOK—Mustad #94720 8x long

SIZE—2

BODY—Braided mylar, flattened vertically to imitate smelt body shape

GILLS—Red lacquer to rear bottom of head

WING—Pintail, single feather, tied in tent shape to imitate smelt body

KENNEBAGO SMELT

HOOK—Mustad #94720 8x long

SIZES—2-4-6-8 (for tandems use specs as above)

BODY—Silver tinsel, flat

THROAT—Long red, white, and blue bucktail well mixed, extended to bend of hook

WING—Four black saddles

TOPPING—Peacock herl, 4–6 strands

CHEEKS—Jungle cock

UMBAGOG SMELT

HOOK—Mustad #94720 8x long

SIZES—2-4-6-8

THREAD—Gray pre-waxed monocord

BODY—Flat silver tinsel

WING—Bottom layer—white bucktail
Middle layer—yellow bucktail
Top layer—purple bucktail

TOPPING—4–6 strands of peacock herl

SHOULDERS—Mallard breast

BARNES SPECIAL

HOOK—Mustad #94720

SIZES—2-4-6-8-10

THREAD—Red monocord

BODY—Silver tinsel, medium

THROAT—Red bucktail, sparse and long

WING—Yellow saddles over which are tied grizzly saddle hackles

HACKLE—White, tied collar style and full

WESTERN STREAMER APPENDIX

WHITE MARIBOU MUDDLER

HOOK—Mustad #79580
SIZES—2-4-6-8-10
THREAD—Black pre-waxed
    monocord
BODY—Silver mylar piping
WING—White maribou with peacock
    herl topping
HEAD—Deer body hair, spun on

LIGHT SPRUCE FLY

HOOK—Mustad #9672
SIZES—4-6-8-10
THREAD—Black monocord
TAIL—Peacock sword, four strands
BODY—Rear rib floss, rib with gold
    embossed tinsel. Front-peacock
    herl, very full
WING—Soft light badger, splayed

DARK SPRUCE FLY

HOOK—Mustad #9672
SIZES 4-6-8-10
THREAD—Pre-waxed black
    monocord
TAIL—Peacock sword
BODY—Rear red floss, front 1/3
    peacock herl very full
WING—Dark furnace, splayed

PICKET PIN

HOOK—Mustad #9672
SIZES—4-6-8-10
THREAD—Black pre-waxed nylon
TAIL—Brown hackle barbules
BODY—Peacock herl
RIBBING—Brown hackle, palmered
WING—Gray squirrel, peacock herl
    head

BLACK MARIBOU

HOOK—Mustad #79580
SIZES—4-6-8-10
THREAD—Black pre-waxed
    monocord
TAIL—Red hackle barbules
BODY—Black wool, tied full
THROAT—Bred hackle barbules
WING—Black maribou, tied full

MARIBOU STREAMER

HOOK—Mustad #9672 or #79580
SIZES—2-4-6-8-10
THREAD—Red monocord
BODY—Silver tinsel chenille
WING—White maribou, long and full
TOPPING—Four peacock herl

EASTERN NYMPH APPENDIX

LEECH
HOOK—Mustad #79580
SIZES—2-4-6-8
THREAD—Black pre-waxed
    monocord
TAIL—Black maribou, cut full and
    short
BODY—Weighted, black angora yarn
HACKLE—Black, soft and sparse
NOTE—Bend front ⅓ of hook
    upwards

OLIVE DAMSEL FLY
HOOK—Mustad #9671
SIZES—6-8-10
TAIL—Two soft olive hackle tips
BODY—Olive floss, thin
COVERT—Mottled turkey
LEGS—Olive soft wet hackle
THORAX—Olive Australian possum
EYES—Bead chain, colored black

GRAY CADDIS PUPA
HOOK—Mustad #37160
SIZES—12-14-16-18
THREAD—Pre-waxed gray nylon,
    6/0
BODY—Muskrat underfur picked out
WINGCASES—Slate gray mallard
    quill, short and stubby note
    slant
ANTENNA—Very sparse woodduck
LEGS/HEAD—Hare's ear dubbing,
    picked out

LITTLE GREEN LATEX STONEFLY
HOOK—Mustad #38941
SIZES—12-14-16
WEIGHT—Fuse wire .025
THREAD—Olive pre-waxed nylon,
    6/0
TAIL—Olive stripped goose quill
BODY—Light yellow mohlon
RIBBING—Olive monocord
COVERT—Latex dyed green,
    Pantone #382-M
LEGS—Dyed green deer body hair
THORAX—Straw colored monocord

ISONCHIA
HOOK—Mustad #38941
SIZES—10-12
THREAD—Pre-waxed nylon brown,
    6/0
TAIL—Peacock herl
RIBBING—Purple thread, 3/0
ABDOMEN—Seal Ex Nymph Caddis
    Blend #105
THORAX—Hare's ear, picked out
WING CASE—Cut from latex, tinted
    with Pantone #154
NOTE—Tie one white moose mane
    over the entire abdomen/
    thorax, rib with purple

LAMOILLE RIVER NYMPH
HOOK—Mustad #38941
SIZES—6-8-10-12
THREAD—Yellow pre-waxed
    monocord
TAIL—Gray goose quill, short sides
BODY/ABDOMEN—Dirty yellowish
    Australian possum, tied fuzzy
    and full
RIBBING—Yellow monocord
COVERT—Full length, mottled
    turkey
LEGS—Tied from stubs of covert,
    folded back

WESTERN NYMPH APPENDIX

OLIVE DRAGON
HOOK—Eagle Claw #1197B
SIZES—4-6-8-10
THREAD—Olive pre-waxed
    monocord
BODY—Weight and flatten with fuse
    wire. Cut margarine plastic lid
    to shape
TAIL—Dyed green deer body, short
BODY—Olive angora spun fur
COVERT—Cut dyed green latex
    to shape

HELLGRAMITE
HOOK—Mustad #9672
SIZES—4-6-8-10
THREAD—Black pre-waxed
    monocord
TAIL—Black goose quill fibers,
    V shaped
RIBBING—Black ostrich herl, clip
    to 1/16"
BODY—Black floss rather full
WINGCASE—Black goose tied
    covert style
THORAX—Dubbed black rabbit
OPTIONAL—Red floss under thorax
LEGS—Black hackle wrapped
    through thorax. Black goose
    quill fibers for front legs,
    tied slanted down

TELLICO
HOOK—Mustad #3906
SIZES—8-10-12-14-16
THREAD—Pre-waxed black nylon,
    6/0
BODY—Yellow wool, peacock
    herl rib
COVERT—Peacock herl over body
    4-6 strands
HACKLE—Soft wet brown hen, tied
    collar style

FLEDERMAUS
HOOK—Mustad #38941
SIZES—4-6-8-10-12
THREAD—Tan pre-waxed monocord
BODY—Dubbed muskrat and dyed
    dark brown rabbit
COLLAR—As body, tied on as wet
    collar on the long side
WINGCASE—Teal dyed dark brown
    1/3 length of the body

DAVE'S SHRIMP
HOOK—Mustad #7957BX
SIZES—8-10-12-14
NOTE—Bend front 1/3 of hook
    upwards
THREAD—Olive pre-waxed nylon
TAIL—Barred lemon woodduck
BODY—Dubbed equal parts of
    yellow synthetic fur, olive
    synthetic fur, bleached beaver
    belly and muskrat belly
LEGS—Barred woodduck fibers

BOX CANYON STONE
HOOK—Eagle Claw #1197B
SIZES—2-4-6-8
THREAD—Black pre-waxed
    monocord
TAILS—Brown goose quill,
    short side
BODY—Black yarn, tapered, same
    for thorax
WINGCASE—Brown mottled turkey
    tied over
LEGS—Furnace hackle through
    thorax

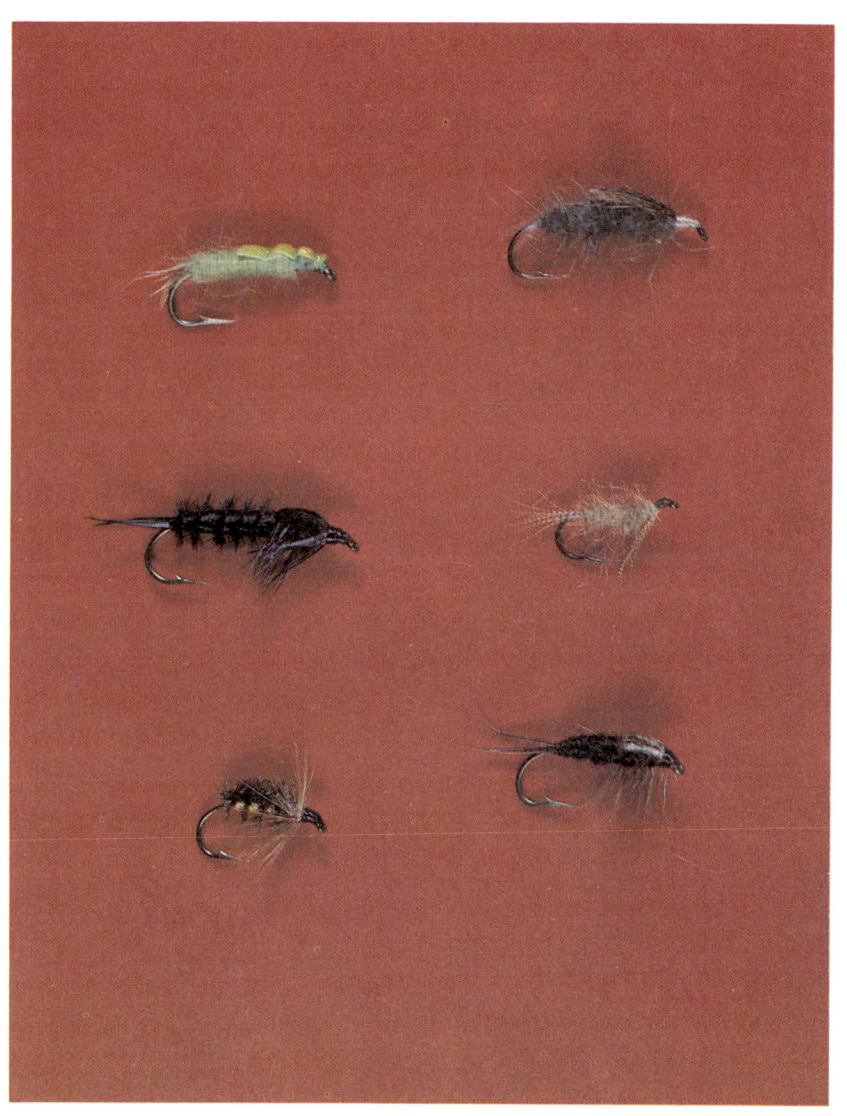

ATLANTIC SALMON APPENDIX

HOT ORANGE

HOOK—Mustad #36890
SIZES—4-6-8-10
THREAD—Pre-waxed black monocord
TAG—Flat gold tinsel
TIP—Yellow floss
TAIL—Golden pheasant crest
RIBBING—Flat gold mylar
BODY—Black floss
WING—Gray squirrel dyed black
THROAT—Hot orange, tied collar style
HEAD—Hot orange

GREEN HIGHLANDER HAIRWING

HOOK—Mustad #36890
SIZES—4-6-8-10
THREAD—Black, pre-waxed monocord
TAG—Fine oval silver
TIP—Yellow floss
TAIL—Golden pheasant crest, guinea over
BUTT—Black ostrich herl
BODY—Rear ⅓ gold floss, front ⅔ green seal
RIBBING—Oval silver tinsel, front ⅔ of body ribbed by palmered green hackle
WING—Two golden pheasant tippets over which is sheathed by green and yellow impali; green is the predominant color
HACKLE—Yellow, soft and tied collar style

ORANGE BLOSSOM

HOOK—Mustad #36890
SIZES—4-6-8-10
THREAD—Pre-waxed black nylon, 6/0
TAG—Fine oval silver tinsel
TIP—Orange floss
TAIL—Golden pheasant crest
BUTT—Black ostrich herl
BODY—Bright yellow floss
RIBBING—Medium oval silver tinsel. Yellow hackle palmer style over
WING—Dark fitch of woodchuck
HACKLE—Hot orange, tied wet collar style

SALMON MUDDLER

HOOK—Mustad #3582C
SIZES—2-4-6-8-10
THREAD—Black pre-waxed monocord
TAIL—Mottled turkey
BODY—Gold mylar
UNDERWING—Gray squirrel
OVERWING—Mottled turkey
HEAD—Natural deer body hair, spun on and clipped to bullet shape head

LOW WATER BUTTERFLY

HOOK—Partridge Sproat
SIZES—6-8-10-12
THREAD—Black pre-waxed black nylon, 6/0
TAG—Fluorescent insect green
BODY—Peacock herl
WINGS—Splayed, cut short and stubby to riffle on the surface
HACKLE—Sparse brown wet hackle

WHITE WULFF

HOOK—Wilson Dry Fly
SIZES—2-4-6-8
THREAD—Black pre-waxed nylon, 6/0
TAIL—White impali
BODY—Cream colored wool
WINGS—White impali
HACKLE—Badger saddles, tied full

STEELHEAD APPENDIX

SKUNK

HOOK—Eagle Claw #1197B
SIZES—1/0-2-4-6
THREAD—Black pre-waxed monocord
TAIL—Scarlet red hackle barbules
RIBBING—Oval silver tinsel
BODY—Black chenille
WING—Black skunk with small
bunch of white skunk
HACKLE—Black soft wet, tied
collar style

FALL FAVORITE

HOOK—Eagle Claw #1197B
SIZES—2-4-6-8
THREAD—Black pre-waxed
monocord
BODY—Silver tinsel, full
HACKLE—Scarlet, tied wet
collar style
WING—Hot orange bucktail or
polar bear

BABINE SPECIAL

HOOK—Eagle claw #1197B
SIZES—2-4-6-8
THREAD—Black monocord
TAIL—Red hackle fibers
BUTT—Bright orange wool
BODY—Black chenille, full
RIBBING—Silver oval tinsel
HACKLE—Hot orange, long and soft
WING—Black squirrel

VAN LUVEN

HOOK—Mustad #36890
SIZES—2-4-6-8-10
THREAD—Black pre-waxed
monocord
TAIL—Red hackle barbules
RIBBING—Silver tinsel, flat
BODY—Red wool (fluorescent)
HACKLE—Brown, long and full
WING—White bucktail

AL'S SPECIAL

HOOK—Mustad #36890
SIZES—2-4-6-8
THREAD—Black pre-waxed
monocord
TAG—Silver oval tinsel
TAIL—Red hackle fibers
BODY—Yellow chenille
RIBBING—Oval silver tinsel
WING—White bucktail
HACKLE—Red, soft tied back
collar style

UMPQUA SPECIAL

HOOK—Mustad #36890
SIZES—1/0-2-4-6-8
THREAD—Pre-waxed black
monocord
TAIL—White bucktail
BODY—Rear 1/3 yellow wool, front
2/3 of body red wool
RIBBING—Silver flat tinsel
WING—White bucktail with a few
strands of red bucktail on
either side
CHEEKS—Jungle cock
HACKLE—Brown, soft and long,
tied collar style

STEELHEAD APPENDIX

DR. SPRATLEY

HOOK—Eagle Claw #1197
SIZES—1/0-2-4-6-8
THREAD—Black pre-waxed
monocord
TAIL—Grizzly barbules, 8–12 fibers
RIBBING—Silver tinsel, embossed
4 turns
BODY—Black wool, tied full
HACKLE—Grizzly, tied collar style
4 turns
WING—Cock pheasant tail, long
and reddish

THOR

HOOK—Eagle Claw #1197
SIZES—2-4-6-8
THREAD—Black pre-waxed
monocord
TAIL—Orange hackle barbules
BODY—Red chenille
HACKLE—Coachman brown, tied
collar style
WING—Impali or white calftail

BOSS

HOOK—Mustad #7970 or Eagle
Claw #1197
SIZES—4-6-8
THREAD—Black monocord 3/0
TAIL—Black dyed squirrel, tied long
BODY—Black chenille, ribbed with
medium oval silver tinsel
HACKLE—Red, tied wet collar style

BRAD'S BRAT

HOOK—Eagle Claw #1197
SIZES—2/0-1/0-2-4
TAIL—Orange and white bucktail
TAG—Flat gold tinsel
BODY—Rear half, orange wool;
front half red wool
RIBBING—Gold tinsel
HACKLE—Brown, tied collar style
WING—⅓ orange, ⅔ white
bucktail. Put white bucktail
on top.

SKYKOMISH SUNRISE

HOOK—Eagle Claw #1197
SIZES—2-4-6-8-10-12
TAG—Flat silver tinsel
TAIL—Mixed red and yellow hackle
barbules
RIBBING—Flat silver tinsel
BODY—Red chenille
WING—White bucktail or white
polar bear
HACKLE—Red and yellow, tied wet
collar style

ROGUE RIVER SPECIAL

HOOK—Mustad #3582 or #3582C
SIZES—4-6-8-10
THREAD—Black or red monocord
WINGS—Tied first, upright and
divided. Usually made of white
calftail
CHEEKS—Small jungle cock on
each wing
TAIL—Orange hackle fibers
BODY—Rear half yellow, front half
red floss
RIBBING—Fine oval gold tinsel
HACKLE—Two turns, glossy dark
furnace

STEELHEAD APPENDIX

BLACK PRINCE
HOOK—Eagle Claw #1197B
SIZES—4-6-8
THREAD—Black pre-waxed monocord
TAIL—Scarlet fibers, tied short
RIBBING—Oval silver tinsel
BODY—Rear ⅓ yellow, front ⅔
    black—chenille for both parts
HACKLE—Black, tied wet collar
    style
WING—Black calftail

NITE OWL
HOOK—Eagle Claw #1197B
SIZES—2-4-6
TAIL—Yellow hackle barbules
BUTT—Two turns of red chenille
BODY—Oval silver tinsel
HACKLE—Orange, full and long
WING—White bucktail or polar bear

KISPOIX
HOOK—Eagle Claw #1197B
SIZES—1-2-4-6
THREAD—White pre-waxed
    monocord
TAIL—Hot orange maribou
BODY—Hot orange wool
HACKLE—Scarlet, tied on collar
    wet style
WING—White calftail (impali)

KALAMA SPECIAL
HOOK—Mustad #36890
SIZES—4-6-8
THREAD—Black pre-waxed
    monocord
TAIL—Scarlet wisps of barbules
BODY—Yellow wool yarn
HACKLE—Ribbing with golden
    badger
WING—White bucktail tied sparse

PURPLE PERIL
HOOK—Mustad #36890
SIZES—4-6-8
THREAD—Black pre-waxed
    monocord
TAG—Silver tinsel, oval
TAIL—Purple hackle wisps
BODY—Purple floss, oval silver rib
HACKLE—Purple
WING—Gray or red deer body hair

SILVER HILTON
HOOK—Eagle Claw #1197B
SIZES—2-4-6-8
THREAD—Black pre-waxed
    monocord
BODY—Black medium chenille
RIBBING—Oval silver, 4 turns
WING—Grizzly, 2 hackles, splayed
HACKLE—Grizzly, tied wet, 4 turns